Real Love, Right Now

A Celebrity Love Architect's Thirty-Day Blueprint for Finding Your Soul Mate—and So Much More!

Kailen Rosenberg

with Jodi Lipper

HOWARD BOOKS

NEW YORK   NASHVILLE   LONDON   TORONTO   SYDNEY   NEW DELHI

Howard Books
A Division of Simon & Schuster, Inc.
1230 Avenue of the Americas
New York, NY 10020

First Howard Books hardcover edition September 2013

HOWARD and colophon are trademarks of Simon & Schuster, Inc.

For information about special discounts for bulk purchases,
please contact Simon & Schuster Special Sales at 1-866-506-1949
or business@simonandschuster.com.

The Simon & Schuster Speakers Bureau can bring authors to your live event. For more
information or to book an event, contact the Simon & Schuster Speakers Bureau at
1-866-248-3049 or visit our website at www.simonspeakers.com.

Designed by Davina Mock-Maniscalco

Manufactured in the United States of America

10 9 8 7 6 5 4 3 2 1

Library of Congress Cataloging-in-Publication Data

Rosenberg, Kailen.
    Real love, right now : a celebrity love architect's thirty-day blueprint for finding your
soul mate—and so much more! / Kailen Rosenberg, with Jodi Lipper.
        pages   cm
    1. Man-woman relationships.   2. Interpersonal relations.   3. Interpersonal
relations—Religious aspects.   4. Love.   I. Lipper, Jodi.   II. Title.
HQ801.R6954 2013
306.7—dc23   2013008061

ISBN 978-1-4767-2796-7
ISBN 978-1-4767-2807-0 (ebook)

This book is dedicated first to my mother.
Without her fervent love for my father and her passionate
and misunderstood life journey (which I often traveled at her side),
I would not be here, nor would I be who I am today.
For you, Mom, I carry the Torch.

To my amazing, passionate, brilliant life light
and unconditionally loving grandmother, Theodota.
My guardian angel in heaven, because of you,
I was introduced to love, true kindness,
and what it means to be a passionate mom, wife, and teacher.
Thank you from the bottom of my heart and every cell in my body.

To my sons, Alex, Andrew, and Jack—you are my light,
my pride and joy, my pumpkin pie with whipped cream on top,
my greatest gifts.
I love each of you more than all the stars in the sky, the universe.
Thank you for allowing me to be your mom.

To my husband, Lance, you are my best friend,
my teacher, my rock, my lover.
I would not know what soul mate love is,
what it means to grow, to be real,
to be strong (truly strong) if it weren't for your love
and your crazy ability to stay on task
when it comes to our life's journey in marriage.
I love you and I thank you.

Last but not least, to my father,
who I wish had experienced more time on this earth.
Your strength, your laugh, your passion to protect,
your memory, and your strong bear hugs remain with me forever.
Thank you for falling so deeply in love with my mom, and with me.
I love you, too.

Contents

Acknowledgments

TO GOD BE the glory and the power, Amen. If it weren't for your voice, Lord, I would not be here. I would not know love, true love, and therefore I would not be able to help others experience the love they deserve through you. I love you and I thank you.

LOVE, thank you for revealing yourself, your power, your truth, your wisdom, your guidance, and your healing. Through you and through many of whom you've shown up, thank you!

Thank you to my entire family—to my grandpa Elton for your constant love and faith in me always and for being my strength and my buddy. To my mother-in-law and father-in-law, Chuck and Caryn Rosenberg, thank you for your love and never-ending faith in me. To my loving family in the "Bird Streets," Gary and Diane, thank you for your amazing love, support, and generous hospitality always. Thank you to my dear cousins Kathy, Kelly, Megan in England, Jennifer K, and the entire "Wilder" family.

My newly found sister, Deanna; my sisters-in-law, Cindy and Debbie; and my tough-loving truth of a brother-in-law Scott, you are loved. Thank you to my niece Julia for being an example of enormous strength and beauty, especially at such a young age. And my nephew Max for putting up with my strict ways and tough love; you are truly an amazing young man. Thank you to my foster parents, Earl and Margaret Hedstrom.

For your never-ending faith, truth, friendship, and support, thank you to my dear friends, my mentors and truth-tellers Dr. Brenda Schaeffer, Steve Santagati, Dr. Keith Ablo, Colleen Needles, Tacy, Alana Stewart, Dr. Paul Petrongaro, Dr. Dana, and Tim Quinn.

Thank you to my soul sisters and brothers—Kristi C, Lucky, Maria, Rachel S, Bobby, Jamie and Scott, Keri G, Susan B, Tammy and Greg, and Paul Carrick Brunson.

Thank you to OWN: Oprah Winfrey Network and my BBC family for being so darn real and such an inspiration, especially Sheri Salata, Erik Logan, Endyia, Mashawn, Karin, Izzie, Bruce Toms, and Jill Dickerson.

Thank you to my amazingly beautiful and talented book agent, Brandi Bowles, and my manager, Steven "The Boss" Jensen. Thank you to Beth Adams and the entire team at Howard Books and Simon & Schuster.

Thank you Jodi Lipper, my incredibly passionate, fun, funny, and dedicated writing partner.

To Joe Miller, thank you for such a special and precious way to enter into the land of love as a teenager. Thank you to Steven Andrews for your values as a true man, your humor, my first son. Thank you, Brage, my sister in Christ who came together with me when the "world" and ego would typically pull us apart.

Thank you to everyone at the *Today* show and *Good Morning America,* to all of my amazing clients at KLLA, and to my incredible and dedicated staff.

Last but not least, thank you to Oprah Winfrey, for believing in me, for being so *incredibly* real, for sharing your words of wisdom, for taking a chance on me when it came to bringing a small town in Georgia to a place of higher love. You are truly a gift and a blessing to all. I am honored to have worked with and for you.

Introduction

THIS BOOK WAS written for you. You want to find true love or are searching for someone to love, and yet you feel that love seems to elude you. Maybe you're single, recently divorced, or married but not experiencing the kind of love you know you deserve. No matter what your circumstances are, you hold on to hope that love is out there waiting for you. You believe that your soul mate exists somewhere, along with a fuller life to experience and an amazing future. You've searched and you've tried, and yet nothing has changed. So what is holding you back? More often than not, YOU are. Each of us has our own history, good and not so wonderful, our unique pain and heartbreaks that have led us to where we are. Now what if you finally had the answer, and that answer came in the form of a special *blueprint* that would help you see where you are stuck? Your own "love blueprint" that would help you get past your own obstacles so that you could finally find the love and life that you desire? Would you trust it? Would you be willing to take a chance on faith, on your heart, and most important, on yourself to take the necessary steps toward realizing that dream?

I have great news for you! You do have the answer. You are holding it in your hands. And only you have the key that will reveal the truth about your past, help you heal from it, and ultimately allow you to meet your authentic self. It is truly only then that you will be able to find and accept the most amazing love into your life. I will help you do exactly that with my own proven methods that will make you question *everything* you think you know about relationships, dating, about yourself, and about what love truly is.

This book will completely renew your approach to dating and relationships, and more important, it will change the way men and women respond to you. But it will do so by first helping you live as your *truest* self, which is the most invigorating part. This isn't a book about flirting techniques or head games. Real relationships aren't about that. Instead, my approach will teach you how to live your best and most spiritually authentic life, which in turn will help you meet and attract your *true* soul mate. Then I will give you the tools that you need to *keep* your relationship thriving.

While I cannot predict exactly how long it will take for you to meet your soul mate, I do know that if you openly and honestly do the work presented here, you can expect to see and feel a major difference in your life unlike ever before within a mere thirty days of picking up this book and getting started. To simplify this process, I've broken the book down into six five-day segments, for a total of thirty days. At the end of each segment, I provide a "Five-Day Love Reality Check" that will sum up everything you've learned and experienced and all the growth you've undergone so far.

Of course, some of you may not be able to commit to this time frame or are necessarily in a hurry to find love; regardless, take the time and do the work at your own pace. You may have a business trip that you feel needs all your attention, a planned vacation, or you may put the book aside for a few days to focus on something else. This is fine, but keep in mind that my clients who lack the discipline to stick with it and stay focused are almost always the same ones who find themselves stuck in the same places months and even years later. Whatever your reason to put yourself and your love life on the back burner, I encourage you to follow my proven time frame and commit yourself to love for the next thirty days, because YOU deserve the change that's about to come!

As you blossom into your most authentic love self, you will become more self-aware and more open to both giving and receiving love. You will open your eyes to the reasons you may have been attracted to certain people in the past and find yourself attracting and being attracted to an *entirely* new type of partner! This is the same process that I use with my clients at my love design firm,

The Love Architects, and throughout the show *Lovetown, USA* on OWN: Oprah Winfrey Network.

Many people wonder exactly what I do as a Love Architect. My process delves deeply into each client's psyche, history, and personal experience with love. Once I've gotten to the root of what drives them, along with what sabotages them when it comes to love, and I have helped them to see and experience it for themselves, it becomes much easier for them to find and create *true love* for the very first time. I have been called many things by my clients: "reality" coach, happiness coach, life designer, love coach, dating coach, love and life guru, relationship expert, tough love coach, matchmaker, and more . . . The truth is that I become all of these things for my clients by tapping into my heart, intuition, professional experience, and personal history (which you'll learn more about later). Through this book I will passionately take on all these roles for you, too. As a certified and master's trained life, love, and relationship coach, with specialized training in spiritual psychology and addictions, for nearly two decades, I have worked with thousands of people seeking love, and have done so quite successfully on their behalf! Perhaps most important for you to understand is that I've most likely been where *you* are. I have my own story of pain, confusion, heartache, and finally tremendous joy in finding *true* love. So take a deep breath and trust that I absolutely understand the risk that you are about to take by trusting me with your heart. I believe that you will be glad you did!

Sometimes when people meet me they say, "Look at you.

Look at your life. How can you possibly understand what it is like to walk in my shoes?" Believe me, I can. As you'll read later, I've been divorced and a single mom, I went from times when I was homeless, living on welfare with my mother in Section 8 housing, living in foster homes, and experiencing abuse of about every kind to a life that is now completely different, beautiful, *blessed*, and amazing. I have authored a book, appeared numerous times on *Today* and *Good Morning America*, have had the honor of working with Oprah Winfrey, starred on a television show focused on love, and been on the cover of and contribute advice to *many* magazines and well-known blogs. After believing for many years that love wouldn't exist for me, or especially that I did not deserve love, I now have an amazing, loving husband and, *most* important, a loving relationship with myself, and I believe in love for me!

I have known since an early age that my mission was to help others find and celebrate love, and I am living proof that if you truly love yourself and genuinely spread love to others, your greatest dreams really can and do come true. I understand what it is to hope, dream, and struggle in life and in love, and yet I would argue that some of us are simply not hoping and dreaming enough. Your most authentic self isn't afraid to be vulnerable or to express that inner sense of wonder that love can bring. And once you transform into your *true* self, you'll be amazed that the search for love no longer seems so hard.

There's no denying that the number of single people continues to grow each year. In fact, there are more than 100 million singles in this country alone, all looking for love. That number includes those who have never married as well as those who are divorced or widowed. Staying single is an option for some. Other couples are happy to continue dating indefinitely, or so they claim, but the commitment of marriage is still the goal for most people. Unfortunately, too many of them become so desperate and fearful that they disconnect from their true selves, veer off God's path for them, and ignore what their inner—"love"—voice is telling them, their authentic self. When they do eventually settle down, they make bad choices. As we all know, half of all marriages fail. The divorce rate, along with the number of painful relationships, is glaring evidence of the disconnect between ourselves and our true souls' voice, and this disconnect is the greatest obstacle to experiencing real, lasting love, especially with ourselves.

This disconnect exists because most of us have never learned or were definitely never lovingly taught how to listen to or trust our inner voices when it comes to love. Instead, dysfunction, fear, societal pressures, and our dependence on social media create images of love that have more to do with ego than with our true souls' desires. Too often, our lives revolve around hundreds of shallow connections and few authentic relationships. This is why I don't simply match two people together. Instead, I match people with *themselves* first, so they can experience the richness and fullness of who they *really* are! Luckily, I have been blessed with the opportunity and ability to help thousands of clients tap into their own truths and find their soul mates! I simply help people get *love-ready* by putting their false egos and bad dating habits aside and strip them down to the foundations of their true *love being,* often their unmet self. Then they can learn to love themselves and figure out what type of partner will be the best for them in the deepest way possible. This is both a humbling and exciting experience for them.

Some of the clients of The Love Architects are people who seem to have it all: education, success, looks, and money. I've worked with chief executive officers, celebrities, world-renowned doctors and lawyers, famous actors, and Olympic athletes. Other clients of mine are "regular" people who work hard to make ends meet. Regardless of their circumstances, each one of them is still unable to find the right match and experience lasting love. Often, they have exhausted leads from friends and family, given up on bars and singles events, and been unsuccessful with multiple on-line dating sites and other matchmakers. They *often* blame some-thing external for these failures. Many women claim that they are too intimidating to men, that men can't commit, and so on, while men seem to believe that all women play games, that there are no honest women out there, or that women care only about bank accounts. Others arrive firmly convinced that their lives are perfect and they don't need any self-exploration, just help meet-ing people who are as *perfect* as they are! This is not the truth. In reality, they've spent years not only seeking the wrong people but *being* the *wrong* people themselves.

Consider the case of Allie, a school counselor who came to see me when she was in her midthirties. She was smart, outgoing, and had lots of good friends. Allie spent her days building up her students' self-esteem, but her own self-worth was shot. She wondered why all the guys she met seemed to be jerks, and she believed that if she could only meet the right guy, she would find complete bliss. She had been on lots of dates but hadn't been in a relationship, and it took me only a few questions to figure out why. Allie told me that other than needing to lose a little weight and "just needing to meet a nice guy," she was satisfied with her life. Then Allie shared that she was a virgin, but that she would often get drunk at bars and end up doing everything else under the sun with each guy she met. It was clearly a way for her to feel loved and in control. Unsurprisingly, she would never hear from these men again.

Now, there is no reason to treat yourself like that if your life is indeed perfect—or even if it isn't. It's certainly no way to find a husband who will love, honor, and cherish you. Allie did not realize that her own behavior and lack of a healthy identity were actually triggering the bad behaviors in the guys she met. I am not laying blame or judgment. Allie did these things unknowingly. But despite herself, she wasn't truly looking for or inviting in the right guy. As I peeled back the layers Allie had built around herself, I found that she was still reacting to the scripts she had learned growing up. I learned that her mother was a hypochondriac and hypercritical of Allie's success. Meanwhile, her father was emotionally and verbally controlling. She had never seen her parents engage in physical affection. Allie was a good girl with a good heart, but she needed to find new relationship role models—beginning with herself. She needed to learn to love and honor herself in a way that her parents never had.

I get hundreds of e-mails each year from men and women who are desperate for me to help them find love. It's telling that even in the tone and content of their e-mails, one can see that they are presenting false egos or failing to be honest with themselves. This is what drives others away. Their hearts are clearly hurting as they continue to unwittingly hold themselves back from authentic relationships. Take, for example, "Carol," who writes:

> *Dear Kailen,*
>
> *Hoping you can help. My friends tell me I make bad choices when it comes to men. I've been in many long-term relationships but have yet to find "the one." I am very physically and emotionally fit. Also proud to be baggage free—I have no ex-husband, no children, or probation officer! My interests include skiing, biking, volleyball, cars, travel, concerts, boating, antiquing, bowling, and live music, only to name a few. I am over all the players and rebounding divorcés making up for lost time. Please help me find a nice guy.*

To begin, from the "proud" belief that she has no baggage, it's obvious that Carol is hiding something from herself. Often, the idea that you have no baggage is the heaviest baggage of all. What is holding Carol back? She lacks a true awareness of self and intimacy.

"Bonnie" from Minnesota writes:

Hello Kailen,

My name is Bonnie, and I am looking for a relationship. I am a thirty-three-year-old, single television executive. I don't have children, but I want to have them. I am attractive. I am laid-back. I am funny. I am fun-loving. I used to be active in the local theater community, and I am outgoing, I am open-minded, and I am optimistic. I love animals, red wine, and philosophical conversations. I am athletic and I love to jog and play golf. I am recently out of yet another "short-term" but serious relationship. I am looking to find the right person, but I am not desperate, because I am happy.

Is Bonnie happy? Her numerous "I" statements, along with her tone, suggest a major disconnect from her true self. She never mentions what she wants in a partner because she's so focused on convincing me of how eligible she is, which is probably what she does when dating. More than likely, Bonnie has become someone other than who she was meant to be, and may have control issues that are holding her back from a true connection. These are extremely common issues that I have seen in thousands of clients who needed my help to find their authentic selves before they could go on to find love with someone else.

The bottom line is that singles are "repelling" each other ALL over the place—online, on first dates, and in their day-to-day lives—and they don't even know it. This is the most basic reason why they are still single or not happy in their relationships. This is why it is *crucial* that you are introduced to your true, authentic self before seeking a relationship. When you fail to do this, not only will you be the *wrong* match for someone else, which will reveal itself later in the relationship, but you will attract the wrong people and even find yourself attracted to someone who isn't good for you. Life is too short and too precious for this, and love is too fun and valuable not to get it right!

I can tell you where to meet men and women, how to attract them, and how to behave on a date. Practical skills are important and will have their place in this book. But you'll never find true love until you uncover the truth about yourself and why your efforts to experience love haven't worked thus far, and that, my friend, will be my focus. I know there is an amazing life out there waiting for you, and somewhere deep inside, you also know this. But you need to do your part to prepare for it. Statistics aside, I am a firm believer in the institution of marriage. I have a beautiful marriage myself, and am grateful to have introduced more than three hundred successful marriages into this world! I believe in the emotional, spiritual, and health benefits that marriage bestows, and I have experienced them myself. That's the life that I want for you! To help you achieve it, I will guide you through the process of figuring out who you *really* are when it comes to love. You'll explore the love scripts that you've been carrying around since childhood and discover why it's crucial to heal from any bad relationship trauma that may still be lingering without your realizing it.

Some of the work will be difficult and some of it will be fun, but the exciting news is that you'll emerge with newfound enthusiasm, confidence, and self-esteem. And your happiness will show! You'll find new love role models and experience love shopping—something my clients really enjoy. Each chapter will include a homework assignment that will bring you closer to understanding yourself and accepting love into your life. In the final chapter, "Be the Loving Kind," I will ask you to accept what I call the loving kind challenge and become part of transforming our world into a more loving place. This is part of my mission, too, and why I take the mantra of being a Love Ambassador very seriously and as a great honor.

When you know who you truly are, when you love and honor yourself, and when you are kind and real in all your relationships, the life you have always wanted will fall *magically* into place. I know this from personal experience, and I have seen it happen to thousands of singles and married couples over the past twenty years. My goal is to get you unstuck, fully aware, and in love. My life experiences have allowed me to tap into a deep intuition, knowledge, passion, and empathy that make it possible for me to genuinely help people who want healthy, whole relationships. It is a gracious blessing to watch people's lives be completely turned around and enriched as they come to love themselves and then find a soul mate with whom to share all of life's joys.

Now it's your turn!

DAYS 1–5

CHAPTER ONE

My Life's Journey

I HAVE ALWAYS KNOWN that my purpose in life was to learn and to teach others about love—what it is, how to experience it, and, most important, how to share it. I've had a unique life so far that has allowed me the opportunity and ability, through continued trials, wounds, failures, and successes, to help make a difference in the lives of others. Every experience that I've had along the way has taught me something about people and relationships, about what love is, and what love is not. I have learned that two of the most important things in any relationship, including your relationship with *yourself,* are trust and honesty. And the only way that you are going to trust me in this process is if you know who

I am. So here goes. My story, like all our stories, begins with my mom and dad.

My mother came from a well-to-do family in Minnesota. Her high school yearbook says it best. She was Best Looking, Most Likely to Succeed, cheerleader, *and* Homecoming Queen. Her successes came fast and early. She had an incredible singing voice, and by the young age of sixteen, she was the voice in many popular advertising jingles played on the radio and was well on her way to a successful singing career. Then one day she met my dad at the local drive-in and it was love at first sight. They fell in love immediately, despite the fact that my dad (as my grandfather put it) was "no good and from the wrong side of the tracks." He had a reputation for being one of the toughest dudes from the toughest part of town. He was also handsome, funny, and extremely charming. For those he cared about, he had a huge heart. If you were in his circle, you felt very loved and protected. My parents fell deeply in love, and when my mother was eighteen, God sent me into their lives.

Unfortunately, his bad-boy image caught up with my dad, and he was arrested for selling drugs, among other things. His background, home environment, and financial stress carried him too far in the wrong direction—right into prison, where I remember visiting him many times as a little girl. Although they were never able to live out their "happily ever after," my father had nothing but words of love and admiration for my mother. Despite the instability of their relationship, it made me feel good to know that my parents had truly loved each other.

With my father in prison and out of the picture, my mother became a single parent at a very young age. Over the next several years, I lived with my grandparents while she was off on a quest to find herself. My grandparents were a true blessing in my life, offering unconditional love, a sanctuary of stability, kindness, and safety in the midst of my mother's unfortunately chaotic life. My grandfather, a business executive and entrepreneur, became my best buddy. In his younger years, he had been a pole vault star at the University of Minnesota, and even made the U.S. Olympic team, but he was left behind when the team was scaled back in the Depression. My grandparents had a lake house in Minnesota, where my grandfather taught me to bait a hook, cast a line, and then how to unhook and clean a fish. He let me tag along with him to the lumberyard and local car lots, where he described all the bells and whistles on the fancy new cars. Of German stock, he was stoic and sometimes gruff, but he made sure that my grandmother never had to struggle or suffer in any way, and that she always had everything she wanted.

My grandmother, on the other hand, was effervescent and quite demonstrative in her love for my grandfather and for me. She adored my grandfather and doted on him—not because he demanded it, but because she wanted to serve him in that loving way. She constantly told him how much she loved him, kissed his forehead, and to loosen him up, would at times tease him to the point of laughter as he tried to keep a serious face. She treated me with the same loving affection. My grandmother was my best friend, as saintly as Mother Teresa in showing me, along with everyone she met, compassion and *unconditional* love. She was an artist and I remember her taking me on long nature walks when I was little, pointing out and identifying the different wildflowers. I awoke each morning to a good breakfast and was tucked into bed at night with her songs and stories. My grandparents were my most consistent caretakers until I was twelve. When I was at home with them, I was most at peace. They loved me very, very much, and provided me with a lasting model of a committed and loving marriage.

But now and again, the telephone would ring and I would listen with a strange combination of hope and fear when I realized that it was my mother asking my grandparents to put me on the next Greyhound bus or airplane to join her wherever she happened to be. My grandparents always supported her efforts to parent me, even though they didn't understand until years later how she lived or what I experienced with her.

I never knew what to expect when I set off to meet my mother. One time, I got off the airplane and was greeted at the gate by a group of exceedingly happy people dressed in bright orange robes with their heads shaved except for a single ponytail, clutching carnations and tambourines in their hands. That was my introduction to the Hare Krishnas, who were among the mix of people at the Ananda yoga camp in Grass Valley, California, where my mother and I stayed for a while. I loved it there, with all the singing and chanting, sleeping in tents with no electricity or running water. I felt surrounded by happiness and the same type of unconditional love that I had experienced with my grandparents in their completely different world. I made friends quickly with the other children at the camp, who at the time seemed happier than any other children I'd met in my life.

But we didn't stay at the yoga camp for long. Soon after, my mother had me tag along as she hitchhiked across the country to join a group of pot-smoking hippies who lived on communes and traveled in a caravan of buses. She taught me how to sing Beatles and Joni Mitchell songs, and her friends taught me how to roll a perfect joint, although I wasn't allowed to smoke it. I was only three. With the hippies, I witnessed yet another version of love, joy, peace, struggle, happiness, pain, and poverty. It was an unconventional lifestyle, to say the least, but until my mother met my stepfather, I was actually doing okay traveling between the wildly contrasting lives of my quiet but loving grandparents and my kind and free-spirited, soul-searching mother. In both worlds, I felt safe and surrounded by love.

My mother met my stepfather by accident—literally. She was back in Minnesota for a visit, and while stopped at a light in her brother's car, my stepfather smashed into her from behind and then took off. Through a friend, my uncle tracked down the hit-and-run driver and confronted him, and my stepfather felt so bad that he came to my mother's house to apologize. As soon as she answered the door, he took one look at my mother and knew that she was the one for him. My mother didn't feel love at first sight. Instead, she saw him as her chance at stability and at doing what she thought was expected of her. Of course, this is not a good foundation for any relationship. My stepfather came from an extremely wealthy and respected family—not the sort of background that would have foretold the years of emotional, verbal, and physical abuse that lay in store for my mother and me. Sadly, he was also an alcoholic, a batterer, and a sex addict, and he made our lives miserable for the next several years.

Despite his trust fund, once my stepfather married my mother, our homes together were broken down and many times almost uninhabitable. He was a rebel and had hated growing up with wealth and the attention that it brought. He drove a rusting, rickety pickup truck with a shell, and he made me ride in the back, even in the winter, with the family dog. My stepfather ruled our home not with his heart but with his fist. If I did something that he considered a mistake, he would lock me in my dark bedroom closet for so long that I often couldn't hold my bladder or bowels. Then I would get punished all over again for making a mess. I dreaded dinnertime, when he would sit at the head of the table with a judge's mallet and pound it loudly if our elbows touched the surface of the table or we spoke with food in our mouths. I was scared at every moment.

My stepfather drank every day, often until he passed out. My mother would get angry, but mostly she tried to pretend that it wasn't happening, as it wasn't safe for her to complain. The physical abuse began not long after they got married. One day I saw her covered in blood. It was too much for me to handle, and I ran as fast and hard as I could into the woods near our home. That's when everything changed. As I ran, an amazing voice came out of the blue and filled my mind, telling me, *"Everything will be okay; it's all going to be okay."*

I'll share more about this story later, but for now I'll tell you that I believe it was the voice of God talking to me that day. Although I didn't know this at the time, I instantly felt safe. I knew from my deepest core that this was a voice that I could trust, a voice that was telling me the truth. I nodded my head as I stood there trembling, alone in the woods, and said out loud, "Okay, I believe You." From that point on, I became convinced that someone was out there watching over me, guiding me along my life's journey, giving me courage and reassurance in difficult times. And there were plenty of those moments still to come.

In the 1970s, society wasn't yet enlightened about domestic violence. After my stepfather's outbursts, the police often arrived at the house to find me sitting next to my mother, who was bloodied and in need of treatment. By the time she'd seen a doctor, been treated, and returned home, my stepfather would have already been bailed out of jail. (His money was a nice convenience at those times.)

His abuse didn't stop with my mother. He repeatedly touched me inappropriately. I would dissociate during these encounters and then find myself at a shopping mall next to him, as he encouraged me to pick out anything I wanted in the entire place. I say this not to sensationalize my story, but to help you understand that no matter what you've been through and how traumatizing it may have been, you can heal and move on from it. But back then, I didn't know this. I felt so very alone. I was warned never to tell my grandparents (or anyone else for that matter) what went on in our family. He told me it was to be our "private" business and that no one would believe me anyway.

And then one day, he was gone. I was so happy! I thought that I would finally have my mother all to myself, the mother who once played guitar, sang "Here Comes the Sun" with that beautiful voice, and had taken me on so many adventures. We went to live at a place called The Farm, a commune in Somerset, Wisconsin, where we stayed on and off for several months. But I never had my mother all to myself. My stepfather continued to weave in and out of my mother's life for several more years. And before long, *she* sadly became my worst nightmare, as she began to blame me for not protecting her from my stepfather, among many other things. Soon her self-hatred and unhappiness distilled into emotional, verbal, and physical abuse, all directed at me. I was still spending time with my grandparents, but I kept quiet about what was happening with my mother. I was in so much pain, and I was too afraid to tell anyone what my mother was saying and doing to me.

You may be wondering what kept me strong and sane through all this. All along, the internal voice that I first heard in the woods as a small child kept telling me that everything would be okay, that I was loved, and that this was all experience I would use one day to help others. As my mother spiraled out of control, succumbing to drugs and the whims of the numerous men who came in and out of her life, I took on a parental role. At age eleven, I would drive on old farm roads in the small rural community where we lived, so that I could get my mother to the hospital after she'd taken too many Valiums and was once again hyperventilating. I was becoming *her* mother, her confidante, her competition, and also her child care provider. (Over the years, my mother had three more daughters. Each of us has a different father.)

The crazy turmoil at home was definitely a well-guarded secret, something that no one had any reason to suspect. I had good grades and dreamed of attending Carleton College, a private college in Northfield, Minnesota. I wanted to be a child psychologist, and I would sit up in bed at night and draw pictures of how I saw my life unfolding. There I was with long, blond hair, dressed in a business suit, carrying a briefcase stamped with the name *Kailen Inc.* on its side. I had an image of a beautiful home surrounded by woods, with a handsome and loving husband and three amazing children. I didn't know it at the time, but I was creating my own early vision board, which I'll teach you how to do for yourself later. I was sure that I knew what my future would look like and I just couldn't wait to get there and see it for myself!

I was only twelve years old when I had a chance to help my first "client" discover her own beauty. She was a three-year-old girl whom I'll call Sarah, whose mother had abandoned her at birth, leaving the girl to be raised by her father. He was struggling to find himself and they were extremely poor. They lived in the back of a small violin shop, where my mother was having my grandmother's childhood violin restored. Every time I saw Sarah, she looked so sad, with a small frown on her face. She wore dirty, torn clothes and her hair was snarled and unkempt. I never saw her smile. All I wanted to do was hold her, love her up, and tell her that everything was going to be okay.

One day I begged my mother to let me bring Sarah back to

our house so that I could babysit for her. I actually had a love design project in mind, though I didn't know to call it that at the time. My mother and her father agreed, so I eagerly got to work. I gently washed her face and her hair, wrapped it in a towel turban, and then held her up to the mirror so that she could see herself. A smile slowly spread across her face! I could see that she felt special. I set her hair in my little pink cushion rollers and we waited for it to dry as I found an old dress in my closet that was just the right size for her. In the dress with her hair sweetly curled, she looked— and felt, she said—"like a princess."

Sarah couldn't wait to leave to show her daddy. At first, this hurt my feelings a bit, as I thought for sure she'd want to stay longer, but I remembered that no matter how wonderful and loved I had felt with my grandparents, no matter how many beautiful clothes, pretty dresses, and fun toys I had at their home, they never replaced my internal longing to be with my own mother. It was an early reminder of the power of love and connection, regardless of one's circumstances. This was also my first taste of trying to help others see their own beauty and feel love for themselves. From then on, every time I saw Sarah, we would share a smile. I don't know where she is today, but I hope she lives in happiness.

Unfortunately, my own life didn't get any easier for a long while. That same year, a neighbor called the child protective services agency, and when our lifestyle was revealed to the authorities, I was taken into state custody and was sent to a shelter for abused children. By then my grandparents were too old to intervene. Over the next several years, I bounced between homes—from my mother's house to an aunt and uncle's home for a while, and then to one foster home after another, shuffling between schools the whole time. As a teenager, I finally landed in the home of a wonderful foster family who agreed to parent me until I turned eighteen. For the first time in my life, I had two parents whom I could call Mom and Dad. Four foster sisters shared a huge, dorm-like room with me, and we had a lot of fun together. I made amazing friends at school, did well in sports, joined the choir and theater group, and met my high school sweetheart. It seemed that, at last, I had close to a normal teenage life.

But in the middle of my senior year of high school, my mother called and said that she needed me. My three half sisters missed me, and she was having a difficult time raising them on her own. By then I had attended at least twenty different schools and was way behind in my education. It was going to take a lot of work to catch up and graduate from high school after having missed so much. It felt like such an uphill battle, and I felt guilty about moving on without my mother, so I quit high school, left the foster home that had provided love and stability, and moved back in with my mother. About a year later, I ended up meeting the man who would become my first husband. We dated for three months and, wanting to do the right thing, got married after learning I was pregnant. We gave it a sincere try, but the marriage was already in trouble and we separated a year later. My son and I moved back in with my mother, who was starting to turn her life around at last, attending AA, and working harder at being a parent to my younger sisters. Our relationship is now headed in a good direction and I couldn't be prouder of how far she has come. In fact, she is on her way to her own wonderful story of healing that is still in progress today.

Life was tough for me as a young single mom, but it felt more peaceful than it had in a long time. I still hadn't found my calling, but I had begun modeling and working as a receptionist to keep my son and me afloat in our new apartment. I started dating again, and I met an amazing man. His love was so beautiful, intense, and healing that it closed many of the emotional wounds that were left open by my childhood. His love and the love of his family were more than I had ever dreamed of, and our relationship felt like a fairy tale—too good to be true. And it was. One day he confessed that not only had he been seeing someone else but that other person was a man.

He begged me to stay, promised that he would get help, and shared his own childhood trauma, but I was devastated and became adamant that I would never love again. For several months, I had no interest in dating at all. It now seemed hopeless that I would find someone whom I could love and could also love me in the pure, unconditional, and spiritual way that I dreamed of, that I thought I had just experienced. And then one night, I met the man who would become the father of my second son. We became great friends at first, and then began dating. Here I thought I was doing everything right. I knew abusive men, and he seemed gentle. I knew struggling men and he seemed confident and stable. I knew self-interested men and he seemed sweet and giving. On the surface, it felt like a great match and in many ways we were, but deep down inside, I knew that a deeper, spiritual connection was missing. The truth is that he was not my soul mate, and I was not his. But I shut my internal voice out and tried to convince myself that what we had between us could be enough, that I was enough, that I was ready.

At this point, I was a successful professional model working for such clients as Target, Pearl Vision, Ivory Shampoo, Vidal Sassoon, and Miller Lite. At only 5 feet 4½ inches tall, I did mostly print ads, commercials, and billboards. The other Target models and I spent so much time together that we were like a family. One day I noticed a sad competition going on between two of the other models while we were having our makeup done. One of them—who was younger and, in my opinion, the prettiest of all—was cutting herself down, finding fault with this or that part of her body, face, and eyes. I spoke to her later and told her to knock it off, describing what I loved about her and trying to motivate her to love herself. She must have listened, because her father called me a few days later to thank me and to let me know that I had made a real impact on his daughter. She had a younger sister who also wanted to be a model but who struggled with self-esteem. He wanted to know if I would work with the younger sister to build her confidence.

As I embarked on my dream of helping people, dueling voices filled my thoughts. On one side was my mom, telling me that I was a failure and would never amount to anything, and on the other side was my grandmother's, along with the voice that I had always trusted (which I now know was God's voice) telling me that this was my calling. I eventually listened to that voice and began to take on a new script for my life. My phone began ringing with calls from clients who had generously been sent to me by this man and others, and I soon found myself running my own self-image consulting business, complete with a business card that bore the company name I had sketched out for myself as a little girl. As I worked on people's outer images, I passionately and intuitively delved into their hearts and psyches. Many were single, and I began introducing them to one another, using my heart and intuition to decide which clients were physically, spiritually, and emotionally compatible. The next thing I knew, the term *soul mate* was being thrown around, and some of them began to get married. My clients became adamant that I had a gift for bringing people together.

Encouraged by their words, I worked brief stints at different dating firms to understand the matchmaking industry and decided that there was a *much better* way to help people find love. Then a writer from *Minnesota Monthly* magazine came calling, wanting to do a small story about a couple I had introduced. That small story landed me on the magazine's cover, which catapulted the company that I ran as a single mom from my apartment kitchen into a full-fledged business with a staff and hundreds of clients. Yes, God is gracious and generous, and he also has quite the sense of humor, as prior to that I had no business experience at all. Soon I was connecting singles across the country, and eventually around the world. I became better and better at helping self-assured yet lonely professionals, beautiful but disheartened middle-aged women, struggling singles, anxious Christians, and other wonderful but imperfect souls of all shapes and sizes.

I've matched CEOs and royalty and single mothers who thought men wouldn't want them because they had children. I immediately found that most of these people were unknowingly sabotaging their own love prospects by never really *knowing* their authentic selves, therefore choosing the wrong mates repeatedly, and acting out broken scripts from their childhoods. I found a way to help them discover the kind of love that they deserved, that would fulfill them by introducing them to their authentic selves first. And that became my passion!

I was creating beauty in the lives of others and enjoyed hearing their magnificent love stories, but I didn't have that same type of fulfillment in my own relationship. I was still with my second son's father, and though I loved him deeply and we talked continually about marriage, I just couldn't do it. I don't think he could, either. I loved him, but I knew that he wasn't my soul mate. After eight years, I ended the relationship amicably. I even promised him that I would find his wife for him someday—and I did! They have been happily married for several years now and recently had their second beautiful baby together!

I realized that if I wanted the kind of love that I was helping my clients find, I would need to take more time to heal from my own past and prepare myself for love, just as I taught my clients to do. I gave myself an honest assessment and realized that I wasn't inviting love in as much as I could. I made over aspects of my home and my life to make them love-ready, as I'll show you how to do later. I worked hard to get past my fear. And then one morning, I got down on my knees and prayed. I said, *"Okay, Lord, I am ready. God, I'm done being a martyr. I'm done being tough and hardened, hiding behind closed doors. I'm ready to love, and I trust you. Show me, Lord, what I need to do to heal."* Later that very night, God sent him.

One of my sisters invited me to go out with her and a girlfriend, and in light of my new commitment to finding love, I went. I was soon dragged into a popular nightclub. I was in a very serious business phase at that time, and stood on the edge of the dance floor in my business suit and glasses, watching my beautiful, free-spirited little sister have a good time, when suddenly a guy across the room caught my eye. He seemed to just float into my vision. As I noticed him, I heard a voice say, *"You are going to marry this man someday."* He was the most beautiful man I had ever seen. It turned out that my sister's friend knew him, and she introduced us. His name was Lance.

Lance reached out to grab my hand, and though I was usually very reserved, I didn't resist. I felt an instant comfort, as if my hand had been in his forever. He led me to a corner of the nightclub, where we could hear each other better, and we talked until the club closed down. We then stayed up until sunrise talking about everything from spirituality to family, beside waterfalls that he insisted on bringing me to, that I had never visited before. Nature is a great inspiration for love, a place to find the stillness inside of you amid the chaos of the rest of the world. Finally, as the sun came up, Lance brought me back to my car and I went home to sleep.

I was awakened hours later by my telephone ringing. It was my uncle, and he was sobbing. He said that my father, with whom I had recently reconnected, had died that night in his sleep. My uncle picked me up to take me to my dad's apartment, which he had moved into just a few months earlier. I had never been there before and hadn't even known where he was living. As we drove to where my dad had lived, I took in every moment, knowing it would be the last. All I wanted to do was to see and feel my father. It felt surreal to walk through the rooms, right by the couch where he passed away. I looked at the coffee table and saw his dinner plate, still holding a pork chop with a bite taken out of it. It was all too much. And then I walked to the living room window and stared out, with tears running down my face, asking God to help me understand why he had taken my father at the very time that he had sent a wonderful man into my life. As I gazed down below me, I realized that I was staring at the very same waterfalls Lance had brought me to the night before. Lance and I feel that it was my father who brought me to the falls that night with Lance, so I could be near him as he took his final breath.

Lance and I have now been together for more than fifteen years and happily married for more than eleven, during which another beautiful son came into my life—our life. Lance is *truly* my best friend and one of my life's greatest teachers. He says that I am also his. Our fifteen years together have been far from perfect. We've experienced intense hills and valleys, struggles that have been necessary for our souls and egos to grow toward a healthy, happy marriage and true friendship. This is what I want to help you find, too—not storybook romance or manufactured love, but imperfect, true, deep, spiritual, awesome love.

My journey has not been easy, from abuse to divorce, loss, and deep depression, but *every moment* of it was necessary for me to become the person that I am today. I hope that through the work in this book you'll realize the same thing about your own story. No matter where life has taken you, NOW is the time to honestly ask yourself whether you've acknowledged your fears and ideas about love and whether they fit with the person you want to be—in fact, the person you already are deep down inside.

HW

HOMEWORK ASSIGNMENT
Write Your Story

Let's begin with homework that I give to my clients to help them grow and heal. I encourage you to take advantage of it and the others throughout the book. For these assignments, you'll need a personal journal to write in, so your first assignment is to go out and buy a special journal that speaks to you. First, take some time to process what you have read so far. When you are ready, get out your journal and write your own personal story about your life thus far. Include information about your parents, family life, childhood, first loves, and heartbreaks. We'll revisit this journal entry later on to see how you may interpret your own life differently after doing the remainder of the work in this book. You will be surprised by how much you learn about yourself and how differently you begin to see your life and love.

CHAPTER TWO

Real Love Is Out There

MANY OF MY clients come to me completely disillusioned about love. Either they have been searching for love in vain for so long that they feel it's no longer worth it, or they have been in and out of so many unhappy relationships that they've come to question whether or not true love really exists at all. They believe that if they haven't found it after all this time, maybe it isn't even out there. But after spending time with these clients and getting to know them, it becomes clear to me and to them that they know very well that love exists. They even experience it on a daily basis, in the form of love for their children, friends, family, pets, or even hobbies. These clients wrongly assume that love for a spouse or partner is inherently different from the love that they already possess. But love is simply love and it does exist, in its purest form, all around us.

The people who wonder whether or not love exists don't really know what to look for when they are out there searching for love. Most of them, as discussed prior, unknowingly hold airbrushed images in their minds from television and movies—romanticized, artificial, constructed versions of love—and dismiss anything that doesn't resemble this as simply not being love at all. But they have it completely backward. It is the images of love that we see in the media that don't resemble love at all, not the other way around. We simply need to learn more about what love *really* is so that we can recognize it in our own lives and open ourselves up to its power.

Another reason that so many in our society don't believe in love is that too many of us associate love with our experiences of brokenness. In our minds, we many times connect love with our wounded egos and our most painful moments. If your stable parents told you that they were committed for life and then filed for divorce when you were away at college, you may have come to associate love with distrust and the destruction of your safe childhood home and memories. If your high school sweetheart said that he loved you and then cheated on you, you may have learned to connect love with abandonment and despair. And if all your friends' marriages seem to be dropping like flies, it is easy to see how these associations can lead to paralyzing fears when it comes to love and a complete inability to trust in its existence.

More than anything, my clients tell me that they are afraid to put their trust in love because of the pain they've suffered from *loss* of love. But they are wrong. Love cannot ever be lost. It cannot be taken away from you. And that is because love itself is constant. It is all around us. And—though you may not know it—you have it already! Now, before you roll your eyes, listen carefully, as it will all soon make sense. It wasn't love that you lost when your boyfriend or wife left you. It was simply the end of a broken relationship, one that needed to end before it completely *broke* you, or it was there to prepare you for something better, much better! That is not to say that this wasn't painful. Being left or abandoned can create a wound that certainly hurts and needs to heal, but it is precisely these types of wounds that need to be dissociated from love, because love is incapable of hurting you.

Before we go any further, I'd like to give you my own personal definition of love:

> Love is an amazing, boundless energy, a connection to something so pure, so good, and so whole that it brings healing, light, and joy to ourselves, our lives, our love relationships, and to the rest of the world. True love is absolutely perfect as it is. It is the most healing form of energy that exists. We are all born with it and from it in the form of God's love, and no one can take it away from us. *No one!* However, what ex-partners can take away is themselves, and that's okay, as God knows what He's doing and trust me, God has someone amazing already waiting!

Please take a moment to think about this definition of love and to compare it to the thoughts about love that you've held until this point in your life. It is likely that my definition is quite different from your own assumptions about love. This is typically because of the things that you were taught about love and the associations you have made to love throughout your life. We'll work throughout this book to disconnect your pain and heartache from your ideas about love so that you, too, can see it as something that is purely good.

Maybe you're wondering how I know that love is perfect and whole when pain and suffering do exist in this world. I know that pain exists—again, I've experienced a lot of it firsthand—but "in the beginning" there was amazing beauty. The earth was created by God, with and from love that we were *all* meant to experience and enjoy. We found pain and suffering in the world by disconnecting from God, from ourselves, and from what love really is. It is this disconnect that causes us to look at love with fear, judgment, and condemnation rather than with openness and understanding. The more we look at love this way, the further away we feel from it. Love is always with us, but at times it feels so far away. In order to bring it closer, you must wake up and start to look at the blessings and beauty around you, for you have them no matter what your circumstances, and open your mind to the idea that love can be found anywhere, at any time.

Too many of us believe that love, or shall I say, "the love of our life," can only come to us through one *certain* avenue, but you have no way of knowing when and where your soul mate will appear. Open your eyes and look around! Your true love might be sitting across from you at the coffee shop you're in right now as you're reading this book, or he or she might be pumping gas right next to you the next time you fill up the tank, but you'll never know it if you're not open to this idea. This reminds me of the *many* marriages I've put together just by standing in line waiting for coffee or to purchase my groceries and noticing a lovely person standing in line as well, who ended up being a client's lifelong match! In this world, we are surrounded by love and beauty, ugliness, and pain; it's up to us to choose. When you choose to open your heart and see the love and beauty that surround you, you will begin to feel closer to the pure, healing energy of love, and to the opportunity for love to make its way in through your soul mate.

What Love Is Not

As a society, we hold on to so many misconceptions about love. These are lies that we have created as truths, and the most common one is that love can be negative in any way at all. This is not true, as love is wholly positive and good. It is again our distance from love and our disconnection from our true selves that turn our thoughts about love in the wrong direction. When we start to view love negatively, we disconnect even more, and we develop resentment and fear toward love instead of openness and gratitude. You already have love, but you cannot fully receive it or create it in your own life as long as you view it as a painful, negative thing. Here are some of the most common misconceptions about love and my thoughts about how we have come to associate love with these negative ideas.

Misconception #1: *Love Is Unattainable*

Understandably, yet sadly, many of my clients come to me frustrated, believing that love doesn't exist at all, or that it is somehow unattainable. To them, love resembles something out of a storybook romance that they are always grasping for but can never really have. In truth, love isn't something that you ever have to strive, reach, or grasp for. It is always with us, right there inside of us. When these people finally do manage to grasp something that *resembles* their version of love, it quickly becomes romanticized, overshadowed with flowers and hearts and other symbols of love that hardly represent the real thing. Our egos and past hurts get in the way, and the whole thing quickly falls apart. True love with another eludes these people because they don't know what they are looking for and don't recognize love even when it surrounds them.

Another reason people think love is unattainable is that they believe they are unworthy of love. As you know, this was my belief even though I had a grandmother who loved me unconditionally in the most beautiful way possible. I also had that strong and powerful voice of my mother, who constantly told me that no one would ever love me, that no man would ever want me, and that I was unworthy of ever being loved. Of course I now realize that my mother was projecting onto me what she very sadly believed about herself, but back then I had no way of understanding this. I was receiving opposite messages from my mother and grandmother, and I needed to reconcile them somehow in my mind. I unfortunately and unknowingly came to believe that love must be earned. Since I hadn't been able to earn my own mother's love, I must somehow be unlovable. I took it on as my personal truth that I didn't deserve love, and I bought into this as truth for many years.

Though I believed that I would never be able to receive love from anyone else, I responded by continuing to love others, or so I thought, without ever expecting to be genuinely loved back. Throughout my early experiences with men, I felt numb. I couldn't truly believe it or take it in, and I found myself acting, "acting out," and just going through the motions of love without really feeling anything. I never believed that their love was real because I thought that I was unworthy of love. Along the way, I attracted men who were like my mother: men who were emotionally and verbally abusive and who abandoned me, confirming in my mind what I already believed about myself. I sadly continued to believe more strongly than ever that I was fundamentally unable to be loved.

It wasn't until after I met my husband that I began to realize where my belief that I was unworthy of love truly came from. In the heat of an argument, he said to me in a strong voice and with tears in his eyes, "When are you going to believe that I love you?" There was something about the power and energy of his words that catapulted me back in time to when my mother would tell me that I wasn't lovable. I finally realized that my mother had been lying to me—because of her own pain and the lies that she believed about herself—and that I had been buying into that lie my whole life. This was a heavy aha moment for me and one of many to come! This breakthrough allowed me to finally start on the path to heal my relationship with myself on an even deeper level, heal with my mother, truly let Lance's love in, and ultimately believe that love was real and attainable, even for me.

Misconception #2: *Love Is Painful*

Many of my clients come to me wanting to believe in love, and yet their primary memories about love involve pain. Therefore they believe that love itself can be painful, when it isn't anything of the sort. This is fairly universal among those who yearn to experience the fullness of love, and this misconception is also pervasive in popular culture. Just think about the popular song lyrics "Love hurts . . ." Or the Spanish proverb that claims, "Where there is love, there is pain." Or Shakespeare's "The course of true love never did run smooth."

I'm sure you can think of moments in your own life when you believed that you were wounded by love, but I will say it again and again: Love is incapable of hurting us. Love can only heal. People who continually believe that they have been hurt by love have actually been wounded by their own ego; the piece meant to protect them has actually kept them stuck. This is what has held them back by causing them to ignore red flags, make bad choices, or accept things in a relationship that weren't healthy for them. I know this is deep, and it's true. While you can certainly be wounded by a partner's actions (or even by your own actions and bad decisions), love itself can never hurt you.

Misconception #3: *Love Is Possessive*

So many people believe that love makes them jealous, possessive, or controlling. I have heard countless clients tell me that they've done all sorts of *crazy* things in the name of love. And how many times have you seen someone on TV or even someone in your own life become obsessive and controlling with a partner, even going to extreme measures to stalk or hunt them down by driving by their home or calling them a dozen times a day? These people often claim that they are acting this way because they simply "love" this person so much. They say it is love that is making them act this way.

I once had a client named Goldie whose husband had left her because he was so sick of her control antics and insecurity. She told me that she had been experiencing strange feelings about him, and so she started going through his texts and e-mails, believing that she was doing this because she loved him. I explained that it was not love but fear that caused this behavior. She had a hard time understanding this and it took a long time and a lot of work, but she finally realized that with real love, there is trust. Acting with fear, insecurity, and jealousy is not love, but people call it love in order to feel in control and to feel safe. With her fear, Goldie was doing the opposite of loving, and that lack of love in her energy pushed her husband away and caused him not to trust her, either. With love, there is truth and transparency, which Goldie now knows how to seek in a future relationship.

Maybe you've done this to some extent in your own relationships. Have you ever gone through a partner's phone, receipts, or pockets, jealously wondering whether or not they've been faithful? Maybe you thought that love was at the heart of this behavior, but if you find yourself feeling jealous or controlling in a relationship, you must know that it is not love that is making you feel this way. Once again, it is your ego and your own unhealed insecurities that are causing these negative actions and emotions. Really, it's a lack of love and connection with yourself. Love itself would never make you feel insecure and powerless. Instead, when you become open to love, it will make you feel stronger than ever before. When you find yourself acting in a vindictive or jealous way, you are not acting with love. Too many of us were never taught how to act with love in a way that honors ourselves. When we disconnect by not honoring ourselves in our relationships, we behave in jealous, possessive, and controlling ways. This is the very *opposite* of what love should be.

Misconception #4: *Love Demands Perfection*

Many people believe it is their faults that keep them from finding love. They tell me that if only they had a perfect body, or they didn't have that past relationship baggage or certain personality quirks, sadly, even children, it would be so much easier for them to find love. Of course this is not the case. God loves all of us already *just as we are,* and we are all equally lovable. Until we can get to the point of even believing this, it's going to be a long road, and it's going to be even more difficult for someone else, especially the *right* one, to see just how lovable we really are. There is no need to change ourselves or especially pretend to be someone else in order to be deserving of love. You deserve love already! The only things that can keep you from love are a lack of openness, a broken ego, or a soul wound that hasn't healed. Even these don't keep you from being loved—they simply prevent you from feeling it, experiencing it, and accepting it in your life.

Then there are the people who allow their own search for perfection to prevent them from accepting love. Take, for example, the story of a client of mine whom I'll call Mary. She came to me in the hope that I would find her a husband. Mary is a successful woman in her early forties who has never been married. When she was growing up, Mary's father was a prominent political figure, but he was a diagnosed schizophrenic and suffered from a multiple personality disorder. These alternate personalities would come out only in private; while in public he retained a spotless reputation. Meanwhile, Mary's mother was an alcoholic. Needless to say, her home life was pretty chaotic when she was a child.

As a result, Mary grew up believing that she must be perfect herself in order to keep the peace and not cause any additional conflicts around the house. This need for perfection extended into every part of her life. Mary felt that she needed to have perfect grades, perfect looks, a perfect body, a perfect social life, and on and on. Basically, she felt that her duty was to keep quiet, cause no problems, be perfect, and keep the peace. That is quite a lot of pressure for any young girl to handle! Mary's father was at times very nurturing, but she never knew which father she would come home to—the loving dad who doted on her or someone who didn't even recognize his own daughter.

Mary continued to seek perfection throughout her life and became quite successful as a result. However, her ego has become overgrown in order to compensate for the hurt that she experienced in her childhood. She now actually believes that she is perfect, and she expects to find the same perfection in a mate. Of course, no one is really perfect. All the men she meets are perfectly imperfect in some way, but when they show the slightest sign of humanity, Mary instantly rejects them. Her search for perfection in herself and others has kept love at a distance, because it has prevented her from living as her authentic self. There is no man out there who is perfect enough for her, and she will not be able to accept love until she comes to terms with her true self, accepts her flaws, and stops blaming others for being imperfect. Mary learned as a child that she must be perfect in order to be loved, and she has been projecting that belief onto the men in her life ever since. My goal is to help Mary understand where this lie came from and teach her that she does not need to be perfect in order to be loved. Only then will she be able to live more authentically and find real, perfectly imperfect love.

I had a positive experience with Mary when I conducted a home visit to assess her love readiness. (I'll show you how to do the same thing for yourself later on in the book!) Before I got there, Mary had told me how proud she was of her home, how comfortable it was, and how much she loved to entertain. But when I walked in the door, I knew that I would never want to spend time there if given the choice! Her house was beautiful, but it was completely cold and sterile, with no signs of life or vitality anywhere. No matter how pretty it would have looked in a photograph, it was no place for love and it did not honor Mary. There was no color on the walls, no flowers to look at or candles to smell, no personal items to be found anywhere.

When I told Mary how I felt, she was offended at first (ego), but she soon agreed with me. She realized that her home revealed a disconnect from her true self, from her femininity. I sent her out to buy candles in a scent that she could connect to each day as she lit them. I had her buy herself fresh flowers each week as a way of expressing love for herself and her femininity. Then I sent her out to galleries to find a piece of art that spoke to her soul. She picked out a beautiful, muted image of a woman with a meditative energy that really transformed the home. When she called me after doing all this, she was absolutely giddy and excited about how much she loved her "new" home. These personal touches lit her up and show how small changes can really shift the energy around you. Mary is still healing from her multiple childhood wounds, but she is connecting more and more with her true self and learning to welcome love into her life.

Misconception #5: *Love Is Vain*

My clients are some of the most beautiful, accomplished, and successful people in the world, and even they often believe that if only they had *more* money in the bank, a *more* perfect body, or a cooler car, then they would be able to find love. This could not be *further* from the truth. Love is not judgmental! Love is not vain. Love does not care about the size of your paycheck, the size of your body, or the size or brand of your clothes. These things have nothing to do with your ability to love and be loved, or even how attractive you appear to others when it comes to love. You are already capable of loving. You are already loved. And it is the acceptance of the love that is already living inside of you that will make you more attractive and radiant to others.

Think about all the beautiful, talented, rich, and successful actors in Hollywood. They are people whom most women envy and most men would love to know. But despite all their beauty and success, they still suffer the loss of marriages and failed relationships. If you could find love by simply being more beautiful, then women like this would have no trouble in love, and all the women in Hollywood with access to the most men and the best beauty experts and plastic surgeons would have the happiest relationships in the world. They don't. I have worked with many celebrities as my clients, and I can tell you that they have the same relationship problems as everyone else. In fact, because it is our egos that muddy up our relationships, people who are repeatedly told how beautiful and wonderful they are unfortunately often have overblown egos that keep them from experiencing *authentic* love. The key is to put your vanity aside along with your ego so that you can meet the real you and live an authentic life when it comes to love.

What Is Keeping You from Love?

I have heard every excuse in the book for why someone doesn't have a loving relationship in their life. This may be difficult to hear, but if you are looking for love and haven't found it yet, it has been because of you. It is your own ego and/or brokenness that has, until *now,* kept you from experiencing love. I say this completely without judgment. I know that you aren't sabotaging yourself or love on purpose, but I want you to realize that your beliefs about love and about yourself are powerful enough to either bring the richness of love closer to you or push it away. If you believe that external forces have kept you from experiencing love, you have created these excuses as truths and made them real. The reading and the work you do throughout this book will help you accept the truth about your own role in keeping a loving relationship out of your life so that you can forgive yourself and move on to find real love.

Iyanla Vanzant, who has a show called *Iyanla, Fix My Life* on OWN: Oprah Winfrey Network, is someone I find very inspiring. She is another example of a person who came from a place of brokenness and suffered through pain and abuse in her childhood. But she did the work to heal herself through helping others and now has a successful television show transforming people's lives and is a bestselling author and respected inspirational speaker. Her life story proves that you can overcome life's challenges if you, as she says, "Do the work!"

In a recent episode of *Iyanla, Fix My Life* she performed a visualization exercise that I often use with my own clients. The goal of this visualization is to find out what is keeping you from love: Iyanla asked a man and a woman from her audience to stand up and face each other, and then told the woman to say out loud every one of her fears and negative beliefs about love and men. After each statement, Iyanla asked her to take a step back, until she and the man were all the way across the room from each other.

The point of this exercise is to show that every broken piece within ourselves that we either refuse to heal or are unaware of, keeps us one step further from the love that God has waiting for us already. Take a moment now to think of the negative beliefs about love that you have been holding on to. Write them down in your journal if you feel compelled to. Now picture each of these fears pushing you further and further from experiencing love, because that is exactly what they are doing. Without even realizing it, you have been distancing yourself from the kind of loving relationship that you want by buying into these fears and lies about love.

Acting from Love 101

Now that you are beginning to understand what love really is—and what it absolutely is not—I want to start opening your mind to some of your own actions that may be distancing you from the experience of love. In life, it is your own actions that either open you up to love or push it away, each and every moment. In

EVERYTHING that you do or say, you are acting either *from love* or AWAY *from love*. Acting away from love simply means that you are letting your ego and unhealed or unrecognized dysfunction get in the way of love. The behavior itself might manifest itself in any number of ways, but the reason you might do this is quite simple. If you say that you love someone but you act unkindly, then you are acting *away* from love. When we fail to honor ourselves by making bad choices or accepting something that doesn't feel right, we are acting *away* from love.

Acting *from* love, however, means that you have healed from your past wounds, or are beautifully well on your way. You have learned to be kind to yourself, honor yourself, and are living as your authentic self. It is only then that you are truly open to the full experience of love and capable of having a healthy, loving relationship. Right now you may be thinking that the mere thought of having a healthy, loving relationship sounds or feels unattainable. I promise you, it's not. Many singles spend hours analyzing their date's or mate's behavior and wondering why they would have said or done something hurtful or neglectful. The answer is very simple—he or she is hurting, unknowingly stuck, and acting away from love as a result.

Many of us don't accept very much if any accountability in what isn't working when it comes to love and blame others for the problems in our relationships, but it is so often our own actions away from love that do the most damage. Acting *from* love means always acting with and in *truth*, forgiveness, selflessness, and respect. My hope is that by opening your eyes to these most powerful ways of acting from love, you will begin to understand how you can change your behaviors in order to open yourself up to the amazing love that is out there waiting for you right at this very moment!

Acting from Love with Truth

When we lie, we're not acting loving to ourselves and we're certainly not honoring ourselves, either. Though it hurts to be deceived, lying actually hurts yourself and your soul more than it hurts the person you are lying to. If you find yourself being less than truthful with someone you love, you need to check deep within and discover why. Why are you unable to honor yourself by being honest? What is it about the truth that is difficult or painful for you? If you are healthy and love yourself, the truth should not be hard! It should be easy and natural. Telling the truth also creates beautiful boundaries that include trust and the ability for growth. This is why lying is such an obvious clue that you are not living or loving as your authentic self. Truth itself contains love and healing, and very often, pain and brokenness can be healed by the truth. A client of mine named Deidre shared a story with me recently that I think clearly illustrates this.

Deidre has a cousin who was like a sister to her when they were growing up. Because of the instability in Deidre's family, she went to live with the cousin and her family for a short period of time. Prior to living with them, and even during her stay, Deidre envied her cousin's beautiful home and what appeared to be the most amazing, loving, stable parents that she could imagine. She was never jealous and only wanted the best for her cousin, but she wished that she, too, could have a family just like hers.

During her stay, Deidre found out that her cousin was fooling around with boys and told her father, naively believing that he was a wonderful dad who would use this information in a useful way. She left their house shortly after, and her cousin refused to speak to her for more than thirty years. All of that time, Deidre had no idea why and ached for the closeness that she shared with her cousin when they were girls. When she recently saw her cousin after so many years, she revealed to Deidre that most everything she believed about her family was a facade. It turns out that Deidre's uncle was abusive to her cousin, her siblings, and Deidre's aunt. When she went to stay with them, her aunt and uncle believed that they were rescuing Deidre from her unstable childhood and that they needed to provide stability for her in their home. Unbeknownst to Deidre, her presence in their home had created a sense of normalcy for her cousin for the first time in her life. But after she tattled on her cousin, her uncle beat her and continued to do so after she left. Deidre's cousin blamed her for this, not knowing the truth about her own life.

Deidre and her cousin missed out on all those years of closeness and loving each other because of appearances and a lack of truth about what was really going on. When Deidre told me this story, it was a great reminder of a very important lesson. When there is pain, you must seek to find the truth about what is really going on. If Deidre and her cousin had been honest with each other back then, they would have been acting from love, but at the time neither of them had the example, tools, or maturity to do this. Instead, they spent so many years acting away from love by keeping up appearances and failing to tell each other the truth. If you experience a similar pain in your life, it may be easy or tempting to rush to anger and judgment, but seeking the truth with kindness and understanding is the only way to heal.

Acting from Love with Forgiveness

When we are acting from love, we are quick to forgive not only others who may have wronged us, but also to forgive ourselves. Forgiveness and truth go hand in hand. When we do not know the whole truth in any situation, we are often tempted to rush to anger, but acting from love means turning to compassion in these times instead. It is the absence of truth that leads us to anger, by creating a lack of understanding. For this reason, many people find it difficult to let go of anger and resentment until they know the full story, but in order to act from love you must forgive first. Once you forgive, the truth will be easier to find and healing can occur, but until you forgive you will be stuck in a place of anger that will cause you to act away from love.

As someone who suffered the abuse of my stepfather as a child, it is still at times painful for me to hear clients' stories of abuse—whether they are the abuser or the one who was abused. It has taken a lot of work for me to be able to go to a place of love and understanding instead of judgment when a client tells me that he or she has been abusive to their family. I can do this only because I have learned that my stepfather abused my mother and me because he was disconnected from love and so deeply hurting, too. It was his own brokenness that caused him to act away from love. When someone is connected to themselves and healed from their own wounds, they don't act in hurtful ways to others. If someone is acting in a hurtful way, it shows the reality of their disconnect from the love in themselves. This is why it is so important to connect with our true selves before we can experience both giving and receiving love with someone else.

Forgiveness can be difficult at times, but it is the only way to heal. When we are stuck in a place of anger and judgment, we disconnect from ourselves and begin to act away from love. There is no room there for healing. The same cycle occurs when we fail to forgive ourselves for our own actions or perceived failures, but when we choose to forgive ourselves, we create a pathway toward healing. It is then that love can enter.

Acting from Love with Selflessness

When many of my clients come to me, they do not believe that selflessness has any place in a love relationship. In fact, many see it as a way of giving up power, giving in, or losing themselves. This is because they do not yet understand what love is. They are still viewing it as a power of ego or a commodity that can be bought and sold with words, flowers, chocolates, or diamonds, or as something that they can choose to give or take away. When I push these same clients by asking them how they feel about their beloved children or other family members, they describe something that is actually much *closer* to the true definition of love. While it is common to perceive the unconditional love for your children as a different type of love from the one you share with a spouse, I believe that love is really all the same. When we are healed from our brokenness and open to love, we can begin to act selflessly in all our relationships.

Selflessness is the antithesis of ego, and as I explained, it is so often our egos that hold us back and keep us from acting from love. When your ego gets involved in a relationship, it tells you that your partner owes you something. You begin to keep score as a means of serving that broken ego, which only keeps you stuck acting selfishly, and ultimately feeling very unloved. Think about the way you show love to your children or even a beloved pet, the completely unselfish daily acts of caring for them. These acts are reward enough themselves, aren't they? Well, the same can be true in any relationship. When your ego is healed and you are acting from love, selflessness with a partner will come as naturally as it does with a helpless child, and you will be rewarded by an openness that will allow you to continue to receive pure love.

Acting from Love with Respect

Acting from love certainly means showing respect for others, but it is just as important (if not more so) to show respect for yourself. I have seen so many of my clients give up too much of themselves to the other person in a relationship. But being selfless does not mean losing sight of who you are. You must always honor and respect yourself in a relationship in order to experience real love. I will illustrate this by using the example of Susan, a lovely young woman whom I worked with on *Lovetown, USA*. Much of Susan's story did not make it to air, so I am happy to share this powerful story with you now.

When I met Susan, she was in her twenties and ever since high school had been seeking men out for sexual attention, always sleeping with them right away. While this had served her just fine for a while, something in her soul was suddenly crying out, "No more!" Susan wanted to experience real love, and she didn't understand why the men she slept with were never interested in a relationship with her. The vixen energy simply wasn't working for her anymore, but she didn't understand why.

One of the first things I did was ask Susan what she had learned about love while growing up. Susan claimed that her mom "screwed everything up" and pushed her dad away when she was twelve. As an aside, she casually mentioned that her dad was an abusive alcoholic, but she stubbornly blamed her mom for their split, because she believed that he would still be with them if her mom hadn't pushed him to get help. Susan gave no thought to what her mother may have gone through in the marriage, and blamed her completely for breaking up their family.

The lie that Susan bought into is that women don't need to be honored or respected in a relationship, and that instead they should put up with whatever it takes in order to keep a man. She internalized this to mean that she needed to "put out" in order to get a man, and she took this to the extreme in her own life by pleasing men sexually instead of going after what she really wanted. Susan and I worked together to come to an understanding of what her mother went through with her father. Once Susan found peace, understanding, and forgiveness with her mother, she began to value herself as a woman and started to show her authentic self to the men in her life.

When we act in a way that disrespects ourselves, we remain completely disconnected from our true selves and cannot act from love. It is when we seek the truth and forgive that we can act with respect for ourselves and others, therefore acting from love and bringing the experience of love with the right person closer to us.

HW

HOMEWORK ASSIGNMENT

Accept Your Gifts

Again, I encourage you to do this homework assign-ment after you have had a chance to process these new thoughts about love. Many of my clients have felt transformed by this exercise, and I hope you will feel the same way.

Start by finding a place in nature, preferably by water, that feels safe and peaceful to you. Dress appro-priately for the weather, as you may be sitting there for a while. If it's chilly, bring a blanket to sit on as well as to cuddle up in. This is a time to be gentle with, connect with, and nurture yourself. When you've found this spe-cial place, close your eyes and raise your face to the sun (or to the energy of the sun if it happens to be clouded over. Cloudy days can be wonderful and peaceful, too, a time for slowing down and just being). With your eyes closed, first take in a deep, fresh breath of air. Feel it fill-ing your lungs with something new, knowing and trusting that something magnificent is about to take place.

With your eyes still closed, slowly exhale and gen-tly think back to each and every moment that you were shown love, real love, especially the love that you were able to show to yourself. When the memories come to you, take a moment to be in and with each one.

Take it in, feel it, and see it as yours, and thank God for sending that love and "truth" of who you really are and *were* to you. Next, thank yourself for being able to see, feel, and receive it. Know that each moment of love was and is a gift, a message of *truth* about who you are, who God made you to be, and what *you* have to bring to this world!

Next, with your eyes still closed, *see your gifts*. They will come to you. As each gift, awareness, or ability comes, thank them for appearing, and thank yourself for seeing them and believing them. Now take in another deep fresh breath of air, fill your lungs, and know that when you are filling your lungs with air, you are also filling them with the love and energy that this earth has waiting for you. If you are waiting for your soul mate, picture him or her fully. What do they look like, smell like, feel like? How do they smile, laugh, how will their eyes look when they look at you? What will you do and share together? How will they treat those they love? Believe in what you are feeling and seeing, for that person is real! Know that they are on this planet at this very moment, waiting for *you*. Now thank God for this moment, thank yourself for believing, and, most important, thank yourself for *loving* you. No one else can love you if you can't. Thank yourself for knowing that you are closer to finding love than ever before!

CHAPTER THREE

Faith and Love

YOU ALREADY KNOW a good deal about my relationship with God and how he has helped me to find and experience the fullness of his love, but I want to talk a bit further about the important connection in all of us between faith and love. No matter what religion (if any) you ascribe to, I believe that faith and trust in a higher power are essential in order to live your most authentic life and open your heart to giving and receiving love.

First I'll tell you a little bit more about my own walk with God and how He became such an instrumental part of my life—actually, the number one love of my life! My grandparents who raised me were very conservative, but there was no organized religion to be found in our family. We didn't pray openly in the house and went to church only a few times a year, on major holidays. To me, church was a sort of boring place that you got all dressed up for on special occasions before going out to brunch, and I had no relationship with or knowledge of Jesus outside of Christmas and presents. It was a very surface and superficial form of religion without any real spirituality.

Meanwhile, my mother was all over the place with her spirituality as she sought to find herself, and I experienced many different religions firsthand during the time I spent with her. As I mentioned, we lived among the Hare Krishnas for a short period of time, as well as in ashrams where we chanted, meditated, and prayed to Buddha. Luckily, my grandparents never shamed these ways of life (though they were so different from their own), and so I simply absorbed these different experiences without giving them much thought or judgment. As a result, I didn't apply any significance to religion at all. That is, until the day that I believe God spoke to me.

As I told you, when my mother married my stepfather, my life suddenly felt like it had been turned upside down. When things became exceedingly difficult and I was truly scared, I would wander outside into the woods, which had become my own little sanctuary, in an attempt to distance myself from whatever was happening at home. That day, out of the blue, I experienced something that I had never felt before, and have only experienced a few times since. An amazing, powerful warmth came down over me, starting with my head and spreading throughout my entire body. It scared me at first, because I didn't know what it was or where it was coming from. But I let the warmth envelop me, like someone had placed a blanket over my entire body, and I instantly felt comfort and peace. Suddenly, I heard a strong voice say, *"It's going to be okay, Kailen,"* and although I was too young to understand what it was or where it was coming from, I knew with every cell in my body that it could be trusted, and that all would someday be okay.

At the time, I didn't connect this experience to God, but I knew that it felt safe and wonderful, and that I wanted it to happen again. In fact, I continually tried to bring this voice back, but it didn't return. It didn't matter. I still believed that it had been real, that it was out there, and that I would hear it again one day. Although I didn't call it prayer at the time, I started to pray to this voice in my own way, and over the next several years I put all my faith and trust in this unknown being in the woods. It provided me with comfort during the hardest times of my childhood, my life.

Years later, when I was in the fourth grade, my mother came to my grandparents' house and said that she was bringing me to see Billy Graham. This was the next step in her own spiritual journey, and I went along, not knowing what to expect. When I heard Billy Graham talking about Jesus, every piece of my being suddenly said to me, "This is what you felt that day in the woods." I had experienced so many other faiths, but I had never connected any of them to that mysterious voice. Suddenly I felt sure that I had heard Jesus speaking to me.

In that moment, I knew that I wanted to go up onstage and ask Jesus to come into my heart. I got on my knees, and as I prayed to that voice I had heard so long ago, I finally knew Whom I was praying to. I cried with joy as I made a vow to God and Jesus to live my life as a Christian. Of course, I haven't lived my life perfectly, which is where God's amazing grace comes in, but my spiritual principles have never left me since that moment. As I put two and two together and connected the relationship I had created with the voice I heard in the woods to prayer, my relationship with God became a very personal and important part of my life from that moment on.

God loves all of us, and no matter where you are in your own life right now, God loves you, too, and no matter what mistakes you may have made or are making today, He sees you only as beautiful and love. God wants us to have the simplest love with one another in this world, but we have to believe in *his* love for us before we can love ourselves and love one another. This is why faith and love are so closely connected, and I believe they are inseparable. It is when we trust in his love for us that we can love ourselves, become at peace with ourselves, and then go on to find love with another. Allowing God into your heart and mind opens your heart to love, because God *is* love.

The last time I remember hearing his voice was during the early years of my marriage to Lance. Back then, we (and our egos) were really pushing each other to see our own ugliness and to deal with the parts of ourselves that needed to change and heal so that we could really feel each other's love. At times it was very difficult and painful, and one day I thought, "I can't do this anymore." I left Lance in the house and went running outside, trying to get out of my own body and experience. It was a windy day, and as I stopped in a field and sobbed, the sun shined down on my face. I screamed into the wind, "When is it going to get easier?" and suddenly I felt that amazing warmth again and I heard that unmistakable voice reply, *"When you trust."*

I cried out to Him in response. Up to that point, I never thought that I could ask God for things, but in that moment I became very humble. I said, "Lord, I need your help. I can't do this by myself and I need You to show me what to do." I told Him that I was putting my life and my marriage in His hands and that I trusted Him. I went back home to Lance and apologized, and even though I was still in a sad place, deep down I finally knew that everything was going to be all right.

Indeed, from that day forward, everything changed. It was as if I had made a pact with God to be my best and most authentic, truthful self in my marriage, and I never forgot that promise. The next time I was feeling moody and stuck in an unhealthy place, something in me was different. While the old me would have stayed in a place of ego and self-righteousness, my inner voice now reminded me, "You gave it up to God." From then on, in these moments I would do a reality check with myself so that I realized why I was feeling a certain way, or I would say a quick prayer in my heart and ask God to guide me. And He did. When this happened, I would often open a book and find an inspiring passage or Lance suddenly would say something powerful and healing.

When you turn your life and your relationships over to God and trust in *His* plan for you, He will call you to a *higher* way of living, loving, and being. A big part of this is taking accountability for your own actions. You can start now by asking God to help you find love, but first you must have a *reality* check with Him. So, trust in the process enough to make a pact like I did, and promise that you will follow His path for you. When you sit down to pray, you can say, "I'm sorry for getting in your way. I know that no other plan for me can be better than Yours, as You created me in love, from love, and only want me to experience love. Help me to stop the pain that I am both creating and accepting." Handing over this power to God is really like handing over your ego; it will end up giving you beautiful and amazing power over your own life.

You can experience this even if you do not already have a strong relationship with God. As I said, I believe that God is that place inside all of us that calls us to our higher selves. You don't have to think of this part of yourself as God in order to let it heal you. Simply say to yourself, "Help me get out of my own way." Ask yourself what pieces of you have been keeping you from experiencing love and write the answer down in your journal. Then push further and ask, "How am I sabotaging my own happiness? Am I being too controlling? Am I acting self-hating?" Am I being too critical of others? Make a pact with yourself to live the life that you were meant to live and to stop doing those things that sabotage your ability to feel love!

Once you have made this pact, you can begin to put out positive energy with the belief that good things are coming to you. This belief can come from a faith in God or a trust in your *higher* self. Either way, when you start to believe, you will feel a shift within you! You will naturally begin to do things that call love to you and keep you on your path. As I have experienced, God loves you unconditionally, and you must believe this in order to open yourself up to love. No matter what you have done or what is keeping you from experiencing love, ask God to forgive you, and He will do so *immediately*. Forgive yourself. God will be happy to know that you have forgiven yourself and that you are coming closer to Him.

You can come closer to God by recognizing and changing your ways. Remember, God has granted us free will and will allow you to go down the wrong path until you believe in and claim something better for yourself. Thank God that the path to something better is right next to you! It's not as far away as it might sometimes feel. You already know where you have strayed from his path. It is those areas of your life that feel uncomfortable or painful. When you are on your true path, it is beautiful and feels peaceful. The moment you veer from it, things will begin to feel wrong. As you become more and more aware, pay attention to your actions, the way you speak to yourself, and the way you speak to others. When you are tempted to judge others, send them love instead. If you sense something dark or disconnected happening, you will know that you are off your path. Ask God to help you get back on your path or push yourself to live more honestly. When you're loving yourself, you're loving God. It's one cycle of energy. Answering to God is the same as answering to a higher power within yourself, because I believe that this is God's voice working to guide you.

How to Come Closer to God's Love

Once you have made a pact with your deepest, most authentic self to believe in God's love for you, and your love for you, shift your behavior, and remain on your true path, there are more steps that you can take to stay strong on a journey of truth and love.

Give It Up to God

As I said, the moment that I gave in to God's power over my life and marriage was the same moment that everything changed for the better. If you are struggling to find the kind of loving relationship you want or are hurting in any other part of your life, tell God that you are giving it up to Him. Trust in His plan for you, and know that when you act from love and have faith in Him, God will never steer you wrong. Once you have given it up to God, ask Him for guidance when you need it.

Find Accountability Partners

You are accountable for your own actions, and when you are on your path you will *immediately* be able to recognize and admit when you have strayed. Remind yourself, "I am making a commitment to myself to make a shift today. I am going to be more honest, kind, and loving." Take this promise not one day at a time but one moment at a time. When you begin to practice this, you will know when you stray and you will get back on track. Your *higher* self will call you back. But it will help if you have an accountability partner who will also call you back when you are straying. This can be a friend or even a spouse, but you will need to put your ego aside to process what that person tells you so that you can see the truth in your own actions.

In order to find an accountability partner, tell the people you love (if they are safe for you to do so) that you are committing to making a shift in your behavior and that you would like their support. Tell them that you'd like them to let you know if they feel that you have strayed off your path, and that you will be receptive to their feedback. During this process, keep in mind that some of the people you seek awareness from may be unknowingly caught in their own ego. Make sure that the people you seek feedback from are people who seek truth within to some degree and in life around them. Then you must follow through by setting your ego aside, and reacting openly and without defensiveness if and when they hold you accountable.

Be an Accountability Partner to Yourself and Others

Calling others to their higher selves is a beautiful way of coming closer to God's love. It is important that you don't force this if someone you love isn't ready, but if you know that someone in your life is trying to be more aware and honest, you can offer to help keep them on track. By sending this person love and positive energy, you will open yourself up even more to love.

First, though, you must be *your own* accountability partner. It is always the easiest and most tempting to lie to ourselves, because facing the truth can be painful. I witnessed this recently at a bachelorette party. The guest of honor was beautiful and perfect-looking and talked all night about how perfect her relationship with her fiancé was, how excited she was to get married, and how much she loved her fiancé's family. But after every shot of alcohol she took, pieces of the truth started to reveal themselves, and by the end of the night she had told us that her fiancé was verbally abusive, that she had very mixed feelings about getting married, and that she couldn't stand her soon-to-be mother-in-law. In the morning, she had to face everything that she had said—all of which she hadn't even admitted to herself! Prior to this, she truly believed that everything was perfect, but now that she had heard herself speak the truth, she had to own up to it and accept it, or not.

It's so easy to buy into our own lies and convince everyone else of them so that we can continue to believe them, too. This is when we really hurt ourselves, but you can avoid it by becoming your own accountability partner and really pushing yourself to find the truth. Check in with yourself daily and ask, "What isn't working? What is painful?" Then you must take the next step and get rid of the things in your life that aren't working! Many of us keep the wrong things in our lives out of fear. We are afraid that we won't be able to get anything better, but part of being accountable means not settling for anything that feels wrong, whether it's your behavior or someone else's, as that is one of the greatest ways that we stay disconnected from love.

Surround Yourself with Others Who Are on the "Right" Path

In order to stay on your own path, you must remain surrounded by others who are living a life of truth and of faith. Begin to pay attention to the type of friends and friendships that you have. How closely are the people around you practicing what you have promised to do? If you spend time around people who are living dishonestly or acting out of false ego, fear, and hatred, they will bring you down to their level. At one point in my life, I felt that I needed to be surrounded by faith-based women, and I eagerly sat down with a group of women at church, hoping to connect. Before long, it turned into a gossip session with the other women tearing apart another congregant and talking about her stretch marks! I was horrified to see this happen in a church, in the name of God, and even ending with prayer. I knew these women could not be in my life and I would have to send them love from afar. You must be very strict about those whom you allow into your life and the energy that you allow in, because energy creates like energy, and there is no place in your heart for anything negative or hateful. Really.

You may have to let people go from your life if they're not living a life that is good for you. Once you've shifted, you must remain surrounded by people with the same personal commitments. It's much like a recovering alcoholic who realizes that he can't be around his drinking buddies anymore. At times in my life, I have had to cut out friends, but it always felt better to have no friends at all than to have the wrong friends. Now when people come into my life, I challenge them so that I can find people who are honest and who will call me to my highest self. In this way, I have found a wonderful group of friends with whom I am honored to surround myself, so I can tell you that people like this are out there. Don't be afraid to let go of the wrong ones. I've had to cut some family members out of my life even though I still love them, and even though this was painful, it was necessary. Part of loving yourself is separating yourself from people who aren't a part of your walk and finding those who will bring you closer to God.

HOMEWORK ASSIGNMENT

What Do You Want?

Once you have had some time to think about how you can grow closer to God's love, it's a good idea to check in with yourself about what you've learned so far. Get out your journal and complete an entry about the progress you've made. What have you learned about your values and faith? What have you realized that you want in a partner? What don't you want? How does this contrast with what you wanted before you started this book? When you are done, read over what you have written and pray to God to send you the things that you now know you are looking for.

FIVE-DAY LOVE REALITY CHECK

So far, you have read about my life's journey, my thoughts on the very definition of love, and the intersection between faith and love. After reading these chapters and doing the homework assignments I've provided, you are beginning to have a new understanding about what love is and what love isn't, along with a new way of looking at love as something wholly good. You are now ready to take responsibility for the ways that you have gotten in your own way so you can move forward for the next twenty-five days and continue getting ready to meet the love of your life!

DAYS 6–10

CHAPTER FOUR

Self-Appraisal

ONE OF THE first things I do with my clients is an in-depth appraisal of the many ways they are both welcoming love into their lives and pushing it away. In this chapter, I am going to walk you through creating the same type of appraisal for yourself. Many people don't realize that the small ways they either honor themselves or fail to do so can have a huge impact on their ability to meet their soul mate or to experience love. I hate to say this, but even something as seemingly superficial as an out-of-date hairstyle, bad makeup, or frumpy clothes can keep you from what is waiting for you. No, not because love is picky about your hairstyle or wardrobe, but because out of fear or a disconnect on a deeper level, you are not loving, living, dressing, or acting in ways that are true to your authentic self. Therefore, the full experience of love has a difficult time being welcomed in! On the other hand, when you take time to genuinely love on yourself and honor your being, your entire energy shifts and you become more loving and more beautiful, which in turn changes your outer image and the way people see and experience you. This is what ultimately opens you up to experiencing true love!

Your Love Blueprint

Part of your self-appraisal is a blueprint that encompasses everything you genuinely have to offer someone else for a fun, exciting, passionate, and, most important, a healthy relationship, both inside and out. By filling out your love blueprint, you will come to realize all the wonderful things you have to offer as well as the things that you need to change. Don't feel any shame in this. None of us is perfect, and we all need to change things so that we can become our true selves and experience the fullness of love with another person. Here I will walk you step by step through creating your blueprint so there will be no doubt about which parts of yourself are in great shape and which ones need to be tweaked in order to let love in. This will give you the ability for awareness, understanding, and accountability for movement toward finding the love of your life.

So often, my clients come to me with a long list of *everything* they want in a partner, but rarely do they take the time to look at themselves, at least honestly, and see if they are at the same level of offering to someone else! Many others assume that if someone has a high-powered job or a beautiful body, then they obviously have plenty to offer in any relationship, but those things have *nothing* to do with who they are when it comes to love. The answer is to create a blueprint that tells us who you really are today—the good, the bad, and the ugly—and where you need to go from here in order to become your most authentic self.

When clients come to me at The Love Architects, I or one of my Love Designers fill out a blueprint for them based on their self-assessments combined with my own observations. This blueprint distills in a few sentences who they are and the shape they are currently in, from the state of their hair to the health of their soul, and that's exactly what you are going to do here. In order to get the most out of this important step toward truly understanding yourself, I suggest that you recruit the help of a trusted friend, family member, or even a friendly ex-partner. It needs to be someone who *really* knows you and is willing to give you their raw, honest opinion about every part of you. If you can find a friend who is also looking for love, it would be a fun exercise to take turns doing this for each other!

Below is an example of a completed blueprint to give you an idea of what you are going for here, as well as a blank version. After you've taken a look at the sample blueprint, make three copies of the blank (or print three copies from my website, www.thelove architects.com)—one for you, one for your helper, and one that you'll fill out together later. Read through each item below and write down a few words or sentences that describe yourself in that regard. Ask your helper to do the same thing, but work separately and don't show each other your evaluations until you're both done filling out the forms.

When the forms are completed, sit down and compare notes, and don't be afraid to discuss your thoughts and reactions to what your partner has to say. You should offer your own appraisal first, and then let your helper respond with the things he or she noted about you. Do your views correspond? Is there something you see about yourself that others don't or something that your helper identified in you that came as a surprise, whether good or bad? You have to really try not to let your ego get in the way, and to hear what your helper tells you with an open heart and mind. Remember, they are doing this to help you, but it will not work if you shut out what they say. If you feel yourself getting defensive, simply accept it and move on. We all have things that we need to change, and there is no shame in admitting your weaknesses here. This is exactly how you will grow and change in positive, beautiful ways!

Once you have gone over both lists, try to come to an agreement on each item and fill out the third form together. Then you are ready to let this blueprint be your guide. Tape it to a wall or mirror in your home, or keep it accessible in a drawer in your desk at work so that you can honor the things that are already working, and also have a constant reminder of what you need to change to attract your soul mate. I have included suggested changes for each category. Ask your helper to be your accountability coach and to check in with you periodically on how you are addressing the areas that need improvement. Hold yourself accountable, too, by going over the items you need to change daily and restating your vow to work harder in these areas.

The fact is, many people have an idea of who they are that is sorely out of sync with the actual image they are projecting to the world through their style, attitude, lifestyle, and energy. Preparing yourself for love includes aligning who you are with *the person you want to be,* at all levels. Are you ready to become that person? Let's get started!

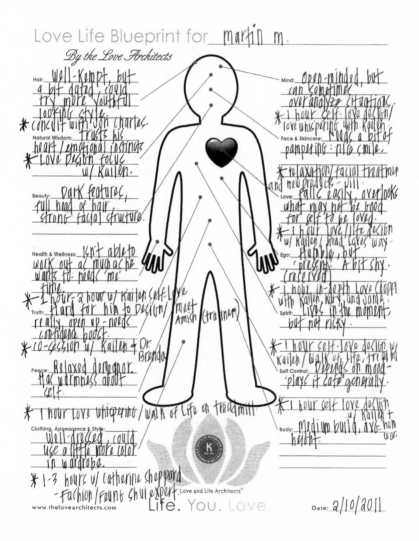

Love Life Blueprint for_martin m.

By the Love Architects

Hair: Well-kempt, but a bit dated, could try more youthful looking style.
* consult w/ Jon charles.

Natural Wisdom: Trusts his heart/emotional instincts.
* Love Design focus w/ Kailen.

Beauty: Dark features, full head of hair, strong facial structure.

Health & Wellness: Isn't able to work out as much as he wants to; needs "me" time.
* 1 hour, a hour w/ Kailen self love

Truth: hard for him to really open up - needs confidence boost.
* co-session w/ Kailen & Dr Brenda

Peace: Relaxed demeanor, has warmness about self.
* 1 hour love whispering/walk of life on treadmill.

Clothing, Appearance & Style: Well-dressed, could use a little more color in wardrobe.
* 1-3 hours w/ catherine sheppard - Fashion/Found Shui expert

Mind: Open-minded, but can sometimes overanalyze situations.
* 1 hour self-love design/ love whispering with Kailen

Face & Skincare: needs a bit of pampering: nice smile.
* relaxation/facial treatment and new products - will

Love: Falls easily, overlooks what may not be good for self to be loved.
* 1 hour love/life design w/ Kailen, Read Cares way.

Ego: Humble, but "present." A bit shy. (reserved)
* 1 hour in-depth Love chat w/ Kailen, Kary, and Jante.

Spirit: Lives in the moment, but not risky.
* 1 hour self-love design w/ Kailen/walk of life, treadmill

Self Control: Depends on mood - "plays it safe" generally.
* 1 hour self love design w/ Kailen +

Body: Medium build, avg hom— height.

Meet Amish (trainer)

www.thelovearchitects.com   Life. You. Love.   Date: 2/10/2011

Love Life Blueprint for_____

By the Love Architects

Hair:_____

Natural Wisdom:_____

Beauty:_____

Health & Wellness:_____

Truth:_____

Peace:_____

Clothing, Appearance & Style:_____

Mind:_____

Face & Skincare:_____

Love:_____

Ego:_____

Spirit:_____

Self Control:_____

Body:_____

Love and Life Architects®

Life. You. Love.

www.thelovearchitects.com

Date:_____

The Outer You

It may seem superficial to say that there are parts of your physical appearance that you may need to change in order to find your true love, but the physical image that you project to the world is extremely important, because it tells the world how you really feel about yourself—and it may not be as pretty as you think. Your hair, clothes, makeup, and even body tell the world who you are every time you leave the house! What we look like isn't important, but it is important that how we appear shows the love that we have within, the spiritual love that we have for ourselves. I know that these items may be personal and at times a bit painful to address, but you won't be able to improve anything until you accept the things that need to change. On the other hand, you may think that you're the hottest thing in town, but if you appear not to honor yourself, and this may come in many different forms, you project low self-esteem or a really ugly ego. Take this opportunity to get real with yourself without any shame or embarrassment so that you can move on from the person you used to be and transform into your true self.

Beauty

What parts of you are truly beautiful? So many of us believe that only the features we see in magazines or on TV can be considered beautiful, but this is far from the truth. You may be traditionally beautiful or you might be striking in your own unique way. Either of these can be equally stunning, as long as your inner beauty is reflected in the way you present yourself to the world. Think about which of your attributes are often praised. Do you have beautiful eyes or a gorgeous smile? Can you accept these things about yourself and show them off with a healthy confidence and awareness of your true beauty, or do you have trouble believing that any part of you could be beautiful? Remember, it can sometimes be just as difficult to accept the parts of us that are gorgeous as the ones that need to change!

I've seen women who had strikingly beautiful eyes but scowled at the world through two narrowed slits, and others whose eyes were quite ordinary but radiated warmth and love. Do you show your spirit through your eyes? Do you have an easy smile or do you approach the world with a frown? You may be drop-dead gorgeous, but if you act nasty and hold judgmental thoughts about others, those thoughts and behaviors will radiate through you and make you *less* attractive. On the other hand, you may not fit within the narrow definitions of our society's beauty ideals, but your kindness and spirit can make you truly beautiful. Take a moment to recognize the parts of your beauty that reflect your true self and then think about how you can emphasize these traits with confidence instead of ego.

Suggested changes: Try playing up a favorite feature by altering your makeup. For example, if you want to exaggerate your kind eyes, try a bit of a bold eye makeup in warm tones. If you feel good about your friendly smile, go for a new, brighter lipstick that goes well with your skin tone.

Hair

Your hairstyle, cut, and color are a big part of your identity, and most people feel a deep connection to their hair. This may be why so many people show up at my office with a hairstyle that hasn't changed since they were in high school! By keeping the same style, they are trying to hold on to a time when they felt accepted, safe, and, in many cases, admired. But times change, and so should your hair. I've also seen far too many professional women who were impeccably dressed and made-up but had fried and unkempt hair or a really bad color. This is actually a form of self-sabotage. If you are not allowing yourself to look your best, then you are not loving and nurturing yourself as you should. Loving yourself means investing in you, and this can mean taking the time and energy to get regular haircuts or to boldly try a new style or product that will help you feel great about the way you look!

One of my clients was a free-spirited, newly divorced woman in her fifties. She came to me with the same bob that she had worn throughout her thirty-year marriage. This is something that is far too common among middle-aged women! I advised her to grow her hair long to better reflect her true and free-spirited personality. She did, and her new style radiated a beauty, energy, and truth about herself that she had long forgotten. She felt sexier than she had in years, and soon all kinds of men were hitting on her, including some who were much younger.

Your hair is one of the first things that people notice about you, and so it is important that it is flattering and reflects good health, energy, and self-confidence. If you have a newer style that you love and that suits you perfectly, great! But if you've had the same look for the past decade or two, it may be time for a bit of a change. Write something down on your blueprint about how your hair truly suits you. This could be, "Reflects my sassy personality," or, "I need to stop hiding behind my long hair." Deep down, you know the truth, so sit quietly with yourself and it will come to you.

Suggested changes: If you feel that you are stuck in a rut and are truly ready for change, try a dramatically different style. A good way to prepare for this is to look through several magazines, both lifestyle and fashion, and tear out or circle the styles that resonate with you and your newfound self! Sometimes small changes can make a big impact, too, so experiment with a warmer color, new bangs, or a more modern take on your usual style.

Health and Wellness

The shape your body is in is obviously a personal topic for everyone. Whether they're in great shape or severely overweight, few people feel completely at ease with their bodies, but it is so important to feel confident and comfortable in your own skin when you are on a quest to experience love. Take a moment now to be honest with yourself and write down the things that you like about your body and the things that you don't like. Take a look at your list. Are the things that you don't care for based on unrealistic expectations or are they things that you can actually change (or both)? Are you treating your body well by eating healthy foods, eating in balance, and getting enough exercise, or are you self-sabotaging by eating poorly, eating too much, and living an unhealthy lifestyle?

Treating our bodies well from the inside out is essential, not just for our health but to honor ourselves so that we can feel confident as we approach the world. The better we feel, the more beautiful our energy will be, and the more electric we will become to others! But if you treat your body poorly, it will show up in your eyes, skin, hair, and especially in the energy that you project. If you're not treating your body as well as you should, ask yourself why you are holding yourself back in this way. Deep down, do you believe that you don't deserve to feel sexy and beautiful in your own body? At the end of the day, if there's something you can't accept about your body, then you can't expect someone else to accept it, either. Now is the time to admit what needs to change, because you will not be able to fully love someone else until you can love your own body. Keep in mind, "thin" doesn't equal love or finding love. Loving yourself and your body *no matter what size you are* and treating it with respect equates to love. I've had women who were considered clinically obese find love with an amazing partner faster than many women who worked out seven days a week who had perfect bodies!

Regardless, if you have spent your entire life trying to lose weight, know that it doesn't always have to be this way. Many years ago, when I had my self-image consulting business, I started diving into finding out the truth inside each person that was keeping them stuck. I found a way to introduce them to that pain and the possibility of where it came from in a way that didn't connect with shame. I tried to help them find a way to fix the problem and take pride in themselves. I found that as I taught them to honor themselves and truly love themselves, the people who had a few pounds to lose started showing up at my office a few pounds lighter *every* time I saw them! One day I said to a client, "Every time I see you, you're thinner! What's going on?" And she said, "Yeah, it's that *love diet* you put me on!" I realized then that by teaching her who she really was and how to honor and love herself, I had helped her lose the *weight of life* that had been showing up on her body. This "weight of life" can manifest as excess pounds, depression, or stress, but when you learn to love yourself at the highest level, it simply goes away.

At the time, I had just had my second baby and was trying to shed the weight from the pregnancy. I tried to turn the tables and do for myself what I was doing for my clients, and I met with a wonderful personal trainer who had previously been obese. He told me that all his clients drank a shake every morning, and so I started drinking the shake and focusing on the areas in my own life where I was still stuck. I also started looking into nutrition and adding ingredients to the shake. Soon I had more energy than ever before and was in the best shape of my life! I introduced the shake to my clients and they loved it, too. Eventually, I started calling it the "Love Shake," and directed all my clients to drink it every morning for breakfast. I'll include the recipe so that you can try it for yourself!

Most important, when you truly love yourself, the excess weight will start to drop off. I have now helped hundreds of my clients lose weight through self-love, and you can do it, too. As soon as you start thinking differently, acting differently, and therefore reacting differently to daily stresses, you will find yourself making better choices when it comes to food and exercise. It may seem obvious, but it's important to emphasize this truth.

One of my most memorable clients was a woman named Amber, who was severely obese when she first came to me. She clearly had a love for herself as she was, but at the same time she genuinely questioned whether or not I would be able to find an amazing man for her. She knew the reality of our society and that it might be difficult to find someone who would see past her excess weight to the beautiful person within. I saw that beauty in her and trusted my inner voice that was telling me I could find her soul mate. Soon after, a fit, young, handsome doctor named Ian came in looking to be matched with his soul mate. When I asked what he was looking for in a woman, he said that he cared about health and being in shape, but there was nothing superficial in his response. Instead of saying, "I need her to be this dress size or that weight," he just said, "It's important that she cares for her body." I could tell that everything he said was from the heart, and he had a wonderful, kind energy about him.

When Ian described the personality and values that he wanted in a woman, they fit perfectly with Amber. As I talked to him, I couldn't get her out of my mind. I finally said to him, "What if I told you that I had your soul mate, but she wasn't necessarily in shape?" He said okay, so I continued to test him. "What if she was overweight? What if she was very overweight?" Ian's response was very sweet and humble, and he said that he would be happy to meet her. He and Amber went on one date, fell in love, and have been together ever since. In fact, I had the honor of attending their wedding more than fifteen years ago. Throughout their relationship, Amber has lost a lot of weight. Although she was a confident businesswoman before meeting Ian, there was a reason that she was so overweight. After experiencing love of the highest kind and welcoming love in, she automatically started to shed the weight of life that had shown up on her body.

Amber's story illustrates not only how honoring and loving yourself will show up on your body but how unimportant superficiality is when looking for your soul mate. Ian didn't picture his soul mate being obese, but he fell in love with Amber on a deeper level and the love they shared transformed her into a healthier body and soul.

Suggested changes: To help you get started on a healthier path, I am going to share my recipe for the Love Shake. Start to incorporate this into your daily routine as your breakfast, and see how good it feels to honor your body first thing in the morning. Then take the next step and start to be mindful of your physical health all day long. I promise that by loving yourself, your life *weight* problems will start to improve, and you will be so much closer to the person you were meant to be.

The Love Shake

1 cup skim, almond, or
   rice milk
1 tablespoon peanut
   butter or sunflower
   butter
½ cup frozen
   blueberries
½ banana
2 tablespoons ground
   flaxseeds

2 tablespoons
   flaxseed oil
1 teaspoon bee pollen
   granules
1 teaspoon vanilla
1 scoop low-
   carbohydrate, vanilla
   high-protein powder
2 tablespoons lecithin
6 ice cubes

Mix everything together in a blender, then pour
the contents into a big, cheerful, brightly colored glass.
Drink the shake with a fun straw and take two B-complex
vitamins. While you drink your Love Shake, take a
moment to repeat some positive words to yourself,
say a prayer, and consciously call love closer to you!

Clothing, Appearance, and Style

As with your hairstyle, how you dress is one of the first things that others notice about you. Do you have a clothing style that suits you or are you dressing for a different time period or even another body? So many women either cover themselves up in clothes that are too big and baggy, or else wear things that last fit them in college, when they were several sizes smaller, or they wear things that exploit them in ways that are not at all honoring their true value. Wearing clothes that are too big, too small, or simply don't flatter your body and personality reveals a disconnect between the person you are projecting and the person you are meant to be.

I'll share a personal story with you to illustrate how you may not be honoring your true self through your wardrobe. I never dressed in a way that showed or celebrated my figure, because I was afraid that it would be seen as seductive or alluring, and therefore either keep people from taking me seriously or, even worse, get me into trouble like my mother. I never wanted to portray myself in this way. My wardrobe was always what others describe as too stuffy for my personality. One day I realized that my clothes in no way reflected my true self. Through my overly conservative wardrobe, I was telling the world that I was someone completely other than the person I really am.

As soon as I had this realization, I went to see a celebrity stylist to help me find a new wardrobe that would better reflect my femininity. She brought me a rack of gorgeous clothes that I never would have dreamed of wearing, although they were really quite tame—simple wrap dresses, pencil skirts, and clingy sweaters. At first I didn't even want to try them on, but the stylist insisted, and as soon as I saw myself in these new clothes, something inside me clicked. I was finally looking at my true self in the mirror, rather than the reflection of a completely different person. Seeing myself in this new way was incredibly healing for me and allowed me to finally connect to my femininity through my personal style.

If you have had a similar revelation but don't have access to a professional stylist, you can look through catalogs and magazines for styles that speak to you. You can also go to a local department store such as Macy's and ask for a sales associate or personal shopper to help fit and style you. They do this at no cost and can help you find a style that beautifully reveals your true personality.

Write down on your blueprint what your style says about you. Do you need to get real and start dressing for the body you have today instead of the figure you had before having children, or do you already have a style that perfectly complements your body and personality?

Suggested changes: Don't forget the importance of color! So many women dress in black because they see it as "slimming," but adding color and feminine patterns are much more lively and attractive, plus they create great energy. Invest in a few new items in your favorite colors and pair them with your black pieces to create a whole new look. Nothing has to be expensive. You can find great things at thrift shops, just as you can on sale at Macy's or full price at Bergdorf's.

Face and Skin Care

Everyone needs a little self-pampering, men and women alike. This is part of loving and honoring yourself. In fact, my clients' bathroom drawers or vanities are often the first places I look to see just how they are nurturing themselves . . . or not. The simple act of applying lotion to your face and body can be very healing and nurturing, and if you haven't been taking the time to do this, it's time to figure out why. Are you so disconnected from your body that it is painful for you to do this, or have you simply been too busy and neglectful? Either way, it's essential that you take some time each day to nurture your body—why not do it in a way that will make your skin feel soft and your face start to glow? Take time in the morning or evening to give your face some attention with a nice cleanser and lotion in a scent that you love, massaging your skin so the blood flows to the surface and you feel relaxed and refreshed.

The same rules apply for hands, feet, and nails. Men and women alike are attracted by well-kept feet and nails, and you will feel so much more confident when your hands and feet look beautiful and healthy. It might sound simple, but enjoying the scent and touch of hand lotion and giving yourself a weekly manicure are powerful expressions of self-love and easy ways to nurture yourself.

Suggested changes: If you are a habitual nail biter, make a pact with yourself to stop this self-defeating habit. You can actually do it. Get regular manicures (or do them for yourself at home) to help motivate you to keep your hands looking nice. Set aside just five minutes each morning and evening to indulge in a skin care ritual with face and body lotions that you like. Loving yourself in this way will help prepare you to experience love with another.

The Inner You

Of course, your blueprint isn't just about your surface. It is important to take a good, hard look at what's going on inside you. These aspects of your personality can't be seen from the outside, but factor hugely in your relationship readiness and in your ability to find your soul mate. Again, honesty is key, and so fill out this part of your blueprint without judgment. Congratulate yourself on the things you're already doing right, and forgive yourself for the things that need to change. Most important, give yourself credit for doing the work and being willing to accept the truth. This is the first and most important step toward genuine growth and change.

Love

It's time to use your blueprint to assess your past relationship patterns, particularly your *own* behaviors that might need some improvement. When have you felt most comfortable in relationships and what has made you *act out* or sabotage yourself? It's crucial that you figure out the reasons behind your own toxic energy in the past. When did you act too desperate, controlling, manipulative, or jealous? What was it in you that caused you to act in these ways? Be honest about what you've experienced in relationships so that you can heal what is broken within you and move forward to give the best of yourself to someone in the future. You will not be able to meet your soul mate until you do this work and heal your past relationship patterns.

It's not all about the bad stuff, though! This is also a time to reflect on aspects of past relationships that you'd love to find again in a new partner and the positive patterns you've enjoyed in healthy intimacy that you would like to replicate in the future.

Suggested changes: Write in your journal about your past relationships and note which aspects of them were the healthiest and most enjoyable. Take some time to also write about your past relationship patterns and behaviors that weren't so healthy. Becoming aware of what you need to do differently in a future relationship is the first step toward changing it.

Natural Wisdom

Most of us have an inner compass or voice that we are able to tap into when we are facing important decisions. Sometimes that inner voice is faint and sometimes it gets drowned out by doubt and anxiety, but it is there, deep inside each and every one of us. Most of us don't listen to our inner voices because of our brokenness and fear, but it is so important to stop and learn to listen to and trust our natural wisdom. It is our true guide. When we abandon that voice, we are abandoning ourselves, and this is how we end up in places and in relationships that God never intended for us!

How well are you able to listen to your natural wisdom? Are you analytical or guided by your heart? Do you have trustworthy instincts when it comes to assessing people? Are you an intellectual thinker or a passionate, emotive feeler? You can gain insight about how you approach relationships by understanding how you view and interact with others. If you approach the world quite emotionally, for example, you may not be able to recognize and react appropriately to red flags in relationships. Logical thinkers may have no trouble making decisions, but often do so disconnected from emotion. When you have the ability, whether inherent or cultivated, to hear and honor your inner voice, you'll be able to assess situations that feel right, as well as those that don't, and end up making healthier decisions. Our inner voice is God's intercom system—his way of allowing his voice to come through to us. When we listen to it, we are listening to God Himself, and so, letting your natural wisdom guide you is crucial in becoming more open to receiving love.

Suggested changes: Set aside some time each day to check in with yourself. You can start with only five or ten minutes and increase the time from there if possible. During this time, sit quietly and meditate or pray in a way that feels comfortable to you. Let your conscious thoughts fade while you access the inner voice that is there underneath the surface. By doing this every day, you will become more aware of that voice in every moment of your life.

Truth

How comfortable are you in being completely honest with yourself and others? Are you able to be 100 percent honest with yourself and able to recognize your own shortcomings that need fixing, or do you lie to yourself to protect your ego from the truth? Do you tell white lies to other people in order to avoid hurting their feelings? If you are lying, you may believe that you are doing it for someone else's benefit, but that is not true. Your lying is about you alone, and is based on your own belief system. If you are afraid to tell the truth, you need to figure out what is going on inside that makes honesty feel so scary.

As you already know, I do not believe that you will be able to find your soul mate until you are living a wholly truthful and honest life. Every time you say something that isn't true, it sends out a shot of darkness that muffles the love around you. I'll be the first to admit that I'm not perfect, but if I find myself failing to tell something "exactly as is," I check in with why, forgive myself on the spot, remind myself about my vow to live honestly, and quickly take it back. I'm only human, and I struggle with imperfections myself, but I have seen the enormous difference that living an honest, authentic life can make. Write down on your blueprint about the times when you feel compelled to lie, and how those lies end up making you feel. Hopefully, this will help you realize how much better you feel after making some changes in this important area.

Suggested changes: The next time you find yourself lying or

stretching the truth, ask God to help you be more truthful. Write down in your journal what you lied about and why you felt compelled to do so. Becoming aware of the times you are tempted to lie will help reveal the brokenness behind your lies so that you can address them, change and heal them, and move forward.

Peace

When you are at peace with yourself, your life, and your surroundings, you generate a calm, approachable, and attractive energy. On the other hand, if your life is chaotic and out of sync, you project a frenzied energy. Take a moment now to think about when you feel the most at peace and when you feel crazed and out of control. What is it that instigates these feelings and what can you do to make your life more peaceful? I'll tell you that you've already taken an important first step by doing the work in this book. As you get closer to becoming your authentic self, you will notice yourself naturally feeling much more peaceful and at ease in the world and within yourself. You can push this progress forward by always remembering to act with kindness, truth, compassion, and love.

Suggested changes: After noting when and where you feel the most peaceful, make an effort to re-create those situations more and more, until you are living the majority of your life in your calmest, most peaceful state.

Mind

It is *crucial* to be protective about what you put into your mind. If you constantly allow negative words, images, and energy to fill your mind, they will be reflected in your demeanor, whereas if you surround yourself with passion, beauty, and love, your mind and energy will shift in a much more positive direction. Be mindful of what you read, view, and the people with whom you interact. Filling your mind with trashy reality shows and hateful gossip magazines can be just as harmful to your mind as too much alcohol or junk food is to your body!

Work hard to focus on the positive in every situation and become more aware of what is going on in your mind. When you have a moment of stillness, where does your mind wander? Do you think positive or negative thoughts? Do you worry, or think only about what went wrong today instead of the things that went right? Do you appreciate beauty and art in the world around you or do you focus on the despair and heartache? Use your blueprint to own up to any weaknesses here and vow to do things differently, such as, "I tend to ruminate on the past or on things that never happen and I want to start intentionally focusing on things that are real, happy, and joyful."

Suggested changes: Cut back on your TV viewing or change the channel so that you are watching things that are more positive and inspiring, like *Super Soul Sunday* on OWN: Oprah Winfrey Network. It may be fun to watch mindless garbage, but it often makes you feel bad about yourself. Find books, magazines, movies, and even television programs that make you feel better about yourself and the world, and devote your precious leisure time to those, instead.

Ego

People often confuse healthy confidence with an overblown ego. This is the time to be really honest and admit whether your sense of self reflects an honesty and acceptance of who you really are or a conceit that was built to hide yourself (and others) from the truth about you. As I've said before, ego has nothing to do with love, and is often the direct result of our disconnection from love itself. When we love ourselves and accept God's love for us, there is no reason to act conceited and we are able to project a healthy confidence that is so much more attractive!

I will never forget Jennifer, a client who came to me with one of the biggest egos I had ever seen. At first, her self-satisfaction seemed justified. She was gorgeous, successful, and very intelligent, and she had a very calming energy about her. I was almost in awe of her until we started talking and she said to me, "I know that you work on healing people, but I am one of the healthiest people in the world. I am completely healed and my life is pretty much perfect. I only need you to find me a soul mate because I know you have access to all the good men." Suddenly, all I could see when I looked at this beautiful woman was her enormous ego! Jennifer's outer beauty quickly began to fade in my eyes.

As a test, I tried to match ego with ego in order to get through to her. "Well, the type of men I represent wouldn't be interested in you," I said. When that didn't work, as she glared at me with a clear look of disbelief, I asked her, "Who are *you*, really?" Sometimes, the truth of those words will penetrate, and sure enough, Jennifer started to cry and tell me about her broken childhood. Her mother told her she would never amount to anything, her father hated her, and she had to build herself up as a result. She admitted that she had been overly judgmental in all her relationships. We ended up working together doing intense coaching for a year, and now Jennifer has found humility. She knows that God loves her already and has learned to truly love herself, and she now projects a loveliness that matches her outer beauty.

Use your blueprint to be honest about your own ego. Did you have to build yourself up as a child to protect you against something painful? Or do you have deep insecurities and a complete lack of ego that has allowed you to be taken advantage of in the past? What may have caused this low self-esteem and what can you do to boost your confidence? Remember that loving yourself is the only way to open yourself up to someone else's love, and there is no better way to nurture yourself than to develop a beautiful, healthy confidence that will radiate from your eyes, smile, and entire being.

Suggested changes: Positive affirmations really do work! The words that you say to yourself are powerful, and whether your ego is too big or too small, it can help to show yourself love and kindness. Stop yourself if you have negative thoughts when you look in the mirror or when you are out interacting with others, and instead repeat positive, loving words to yourself.

Your Home Visit

After completing a blueprint with each of my clients, the next step in the self-appraisal is for me to conduct a home visit. This is a crucial part of helping them become open to love, as it allows me to identify whether or not they are honoring themselves through their home environment. Our homes say so much about the state of our minds, psyches, and egos. Walking into your home is like walking into your very being and tells us everything we need to know about what is going on within us at every level.

The state of your home also says a lot about how receptive you are to love. A cold, sterile home, no matter how visually perfect or well decorated, has no room for love, but a warm, inviting space that makes you and your guests feel safe and nurtured is the ideal environment in which to seek and ultimately cherish love with your soul mate. Keep in mind that this is not about having a lot of money and fancy things. Modest, small homes can feel just as homey as the most opulent mansions. In fact, some of the most impoverished homes I've been in have made me feel more comfortable than some of the most lavish mansions in Bel Air. Tweaking your home in order to make it better represent your personality doesn't have to be expensive, either. As we move through each room of your home, I'll make suggested improvements that are incredibly affordable and will make a dramatic impact. Remember the story of Mary that I told you earlier. Her home was opulent and professionally decorated, but it did not celebrate Mary's warmth or femininity on any level. The relatively small changes we made together completely changed the feel of her home and her connection to these parts of her personality.

Although I may not be able to visit your home in person, I will walk you through the process of conducting your own home visit, and I encourage you to recruit a friend to help you with this. This can be the same partner you used to help you complete your blueprint. Again, think about taking turns with a friend who is on a similar quest to find a soul mate. Make sure that this person is willing to be completely honest with you and that you approach this exercise with an open mind. Recognizing the parts of your home that do not honor your true self is a big step toward becoming that person, and making the necessary changes will prepare you to let love in. Are you ready? Grab your journal and your accountability buddy and let's take a tour of your home unlike any other!

Entryway and Main Living Areas

Start by going outside and then walking into your front door. Stop for a moment and look around with a heightened consciousness. You come in and out of this door every day, but I bet you don't often take the time to really look around and notice things. The entry to your home signifies your arrival at a safe, nurturing, and sacred place—home. How does the space feel? How does it smell? Are the colors lively and bright, or drab? Is the light harsh and disorienting or warm and welcoming? Is the space inviting or is there dirt, clutter, or off-putting odors? If you were entering this space for the first time, would you want to spend time here? Now think about how your space reflects your true self. Does it tell a story about who you are? Does it honor the entrance of love in your life? Does your home contain life? Flowers and plants are living things that bring vitality and energy into a home, not to mention beauty. Do the scents in your home bring calmness and peace? How are you nurturing yourself through your home?

Suggested changes: If you realize that the entry rooms to your home do not reflect your true self, you need to make some changes. If the space feels drab, a coat of paint in a favorite, inviting color is a great way to make a big change for relatively little money. If your walls are bare, hang some family photos or spend time at thrift stores looking for prints that speak to you. If your home needs more life, start buying yourself inexpensive flowers each week. This is a small investment that will pay back big-time in the way it makes your home feel, look, and even smell. Speaking of smells, aromatherapy is very powerful and important. If your home's smell isn't inviting, purchase some candles in a scent that you love. A few throw pillows or cozy blankets in the living room can instantly transform the space and make it feel much more homey. These small changes will be wonderful for your sense of well-being.

Kitchen

Now it's time to move on to one of the most important rooms in any home—the kitchen. The state of your kitchen speaks volumes about how you nurture your body through food. Open your refrigerator and take an honest account of what the food in there says about you. Is it full of processed junk that is harmful to your body and spirit? Is it bare, reflecting an inability to nurture yourself properly? Or is the food in there all meant for entertaining and to serve others, with nothing that's just for you? Look at the freezer, the cupboards, and especially any secret stashes that you may have hidden away. Do you use these foods to self-medicate when you are feeling anxious or depressed? What is the truth that your kitchen says about you?

Now let's talk about cleanliness, which is especially important in the kitchen. Of course there will be times when the dishes pile up or things get spilled, but in general your kitchen should be kept nice and tidy. If your kitchen is consistently messy with dishes left in the sink for days, crumbs everywhere, and garbage piling up, this is a sign of a major disconnect within you. What is it? Deep down, you probably already know. What is the mess inside you that is being represented in your kitchen? On the other hand, a compulsion to keep things spotless at all times may reflect a similar disconnection from your true self. The goal here is to find a healthy balance so that your home honors your spirit and gives you room to breathe and live comfortably.

Suggested changes: Now is a great time to clean out your cupboards and to restock your pantry with foods that are healthy and nourishing and reflect the life you want to live. This can mean getting rid of junk food or buying more of your favorites that are "healthy" so that your kitchen begins to reflect your tastes, as well as your commitment to honor your body through the foods you eat. Keep a bowl of fresh fruit out on the kitchen counter. The colors will lift your spirits and it will be easier to eat healthy snacks if they are right there in front of you. If you have any *secret* foods hidden, throw them away now. Eating in secret is always a sign of something that is broken inside of you. Take a moment to think about why you have felt the need to eat in secret, forgive yourself for acting out in this way, and then vow never to do it again. I'm not saying that you shouldn't ever have Oreos again or your favorite guilty pleasure, just don't hide them. If you want them, place them out in the open in perhaps a big, fun, clear enclosed cylinder!

Bedroom

Your bedroom has a special importance as your nest, your place to honor and cherish yourself and retreat from the rest of the world. Go into your bedroom and think about how it makes you feel. Is it cozy? Warm? What does it say about you? What images are displayed on your walls? What items surround you on your night-stand? Is there anything in here that reflects romance, love, and family? Remember, this space is where your love will ultimately be consummated, and so it should reflect your truest self on the deepest level.

Remember that your bedroom is not the place for photos on your nightstand of your mom and dad, or photos of your ex-wife or ex-boyfriend! I once went into a client's home and found her wedding pictures on her nightstand. She had been divorced for five years! This is not the way to honor your future mate or open yourself up to finding a new love. While you're in your bedroom, take a look inside your closet and in your drawers, too. Are your clothes neatly folded or lying in haphazard piles? How do you treat the items that you wear on your body, and what does this say about you?

I will admit that the state of my own closet reveals a piece of me that I'm still working on! The majority of my home feels like a retreat and is quite balanced, which is very important to me, but my closet tells another story. I have a large walk-in closet that is bigger than my son's bedroom (as he often reminds me!), but it's like a maze, because the floor is covered with piles and piles of clothes. Yes, my argument could be—and trust me, has been— that at least they are clean, but it is still a mess, and you can barely walk through it without fear of breaking a leg. To top it off, there are suitcases in there from weeks ago that I still haven't unpacked. Again, my excuse is that I travel so much for my work. My closet is a discombobulated mess, and this clearly reflects something that isn't working in my life.

The mess is telling me that I need to slow down. The still-packed suitcases, the piles of clean clothes that I still haven't found time to put away, and all the general chaos in my closet are the results of me being on the go so much and never having enough quiet time to settle myself (or my closet)! The truth is that my closet is like this 70 percent of the time. When I can't take it anymore, I go in and clean it up, and then the cycle starts over. It's clear that I'm ignoring something by allowing this to continue, and I vow to take some time to sit in my closet, pray, and think about the story my closet is telling me. Hopefully by the time you read this, I will have learned how to honor myself by better caring for my things and that part of my home.

Suggested changes: If your bedroom isn't as comfortable as it could be, start by investing in some good-quality bedding. It doesn't have to be expensive—simple cotton sheets and pillow-cases should do the trick. Add layers of blankets so that you can cocoon yourself in this space. Replace clutter on your nightstand with a framed family photo. Place more photos on the walls or think about hanging inspirational words above your bed. You will be amazed by how good it feels to see these things right before you go to bed at night and first thing in the morning. Finally, if you have been dishonoring yourself by taking poor care of your personal items, spend some time in this space thinking about why. Reorganize your drawers and closet to create a more peaceful, loving environment.

Bathroom

Cleanliness is obviously an issue here, as are the items you use to nurture your body, skin, and hair. What do you see in your medicine cabinet and on your vanity? Do you have products that you use to pamper yourself, or does your bathroom reflect a rushed, utilitarian lifestyle? If you balk at the idea of pampering yourself with bath products, ask yourself why. I have had so many male clients laugh at me when I said that I wanted them to buy skin care products, but after just a few days of using them, they absolutely loved it. You should see these guys after I talk them into getting facials! I hear through outside sources that they are secretly hooked! Again, this isn't about purchasing the most expensive skin care lines—drugstore brands are absolutely fine. It is simply about the act of loving yourself through touch and care.

Suggested changes: Take some time to find bath products in scents that you love—from soap and moisturizer to shampoo and conditioner. Get some nice, soft matching towels. (They don't have to be expensive.) You'll notice the difference every time you take a shower or simply wash your hands. Clean up any clutter in this room, too. The bathroom should be a place that makes you feel clean and healthy, never dirty or out of control. Indulge yourself by adding some cozy slippers or a nice bathrobe that you can look forward to putting on at the end of a long day. So many people "save" cozy items like bathrobes and slippers for when they are feeling down or under the weather. Don't wait until you are sad or depressed to nurture yourself in these ways. Treating yourself tenderly even when things are good will keep depressed thoughts and feelings at bay. Remember, the way you love and nurture yourself reflects your ability to love and nurture others, and in turn allows them to love you back.

HOMEWORK ASSIGNMENT
Create Your Vision Board

Once you have completed your blueprint, finished your home visit, and are beginning to implement the necessary changes that both these exercises revealed, take some time to see how your energy is starting to shift. When you are ready, it's time to create a vision board that will represent your most authentic self. Oprah first made vision boards famous and much has been written about them since then, and I believe that they are a very powerful tool in becoming the person you were meant to be. By creating a visual image of that person, you will become more connected to him or her and find yourself transforming into that person over time.

Start by going to a crafts store and getting a big tagboard, scissors, and glue. Next, go to a bookstore and buy several magazines that you enjoy reading and that will be likely to contain images of your ideal lifestyle. Go through the magazines and tear out every image that *speaks* to you from your soul. You'll know what I mean when you start. Start with pictures of other women (or men if you are a man) that you connect with. It can be a woman with long hair blowing in the wind even though you currently have short hair, or a woman with a lovely natural face though you now wear a great deal of makeup. They don't have to represent who you are now, but they should speak to the person you wish to become, the person that you believe is authentically who you are but never allowed yourself the chance to be. Now begin tearing out images of homes that you love, places in nature that speak to you on some level, and anything else that you feel connected to. It can be an engagement ring that you might love to wear someday, a field of beautiful flowers, or a serene animal.

After you've glued the images to your vision board, look them over one by one and ask yourself what it was that connected you to this image. Spend some time here listening to your authentic voice. The real reason you tore out a certain picture might not reveal itself right away. When you have the answers, write them down next to each picture as a reminder to yourself of what each one represents to the real you. When you're done, hang your vision board somewhere you'll be able to see it every day, and make sure that you do look at it that frequently, taking a few minutes each day to connect to the images you chose to represent your most honest, authentic self.

CHAPTER FIVE

Love Scripts

WHAT EXACTLY IS a love script? Just like any script, it is a breakdown of the lines and actions that you act out, but unlike a script for a movie or play, love scripts are lived out *unconsciously* based on your internalized beliefs about yourself and about love. Your own love script has been written for you starting before you were even born, based on the love that you were conceived in, how you were loved, nurtured, and cared for as a child, and the role models of love that have surrounded you throughout your life. Were you raised as lovable, without any strings or conditions? Your subconscious mind, which is made up of your heart, soul, and ego, has taken on this script and you have been acting it out ever since in each one of your relationships. Yet until this point you probably haven't been aware of it.

Our scripts are not written and finalized when we are children, although modern psychology states something different. I believe and have seen through trials and healing that our script continues to be edited and rewritten as our lives progress, based on our own experiences with first loves, early crushes, and even heartbreaks and losses. For most of our lives, we write our own scripts unknowingly, based on the things we are told, the ways we are treated, and the relationships we observe around us. Through the work in this book, I want to help you get to the point where you can knowingly and wisely write your own script going forward. This is how you will ultimately find your happily ever after!

Please don't forget that love scripts are not always negative. They are the source of our joy *and* our brokenness, depending on what they say and what we believe. Right now, some parts of your love script may be functional, while others simply aren't working for you. My goal is to help you identify exactly where your love script is broken so that you may heal from it and rewrite a more wholly positive and joyous script for your life!

Very often, people will come to me raving about what wonderful parents they had but wondering why they attract such toxic relationships. The vast majority of these people will later realize that their parents actually did not provide as much stability and love as they could have. Just recently, a couple came to me in crisis. I'll call them John and Jane. John had been physically abusive to Jane and they were on the brink of divorce. When I asked John about his parents, he started by saying that they were supportive and loving, but as I asked more questions, he revealed that his father was abusive to his mother, as well. I then asked Jane about her parents, and she said that she did not understand how she could have ended up (and stayed) in a relationship like this because her father had been so lovely and gentle. I said, "What about your mother?" and she revealed that her mother was shaming and cruel to Jane as a child. Many people think that they'll marry a partner like their parent of the opposite sex, but that isn't always the case! The words and actions of both parents have a place in your own love script. It was clear to me that Jane and John both had broken love scripts that led to the state of their marriage. If they had grown up witnessing a healthy dynamic of love and were taught to love themselves, they might still have fallen in love or lust with someone who was disconnected from their healthier self, but they wouldn't have stayed in that relationship. The people who stay in toxic relationships have soul wounds that can only come from a broken love script. In my many years as a Love Architect, I have interviewed thousands of people on a deep level, and from this experience I have discovered *seven* of the most common "broken" love scripts. You can think of these as the seven deadly scripts! As you read through them, I want you to think about which parts of these stories you relate to so that you can begin to understand the way your own love script was written and how you might be able to rewrite it in a more positive and healthy way.

Broken Love Script #1: *I Have No Value When It Comes to Love*

Many negative love scripts tell us that we have little or no true value beyond what our ego identifies with, and these scripts can manifest themselves in various ways depending on exactly what we saw and were told as a child. A woman named Amy who was successful in every aspect of her life except for love once came to me. She couldn't understand why she continued to attract abusive, condescending men who treated her badly. Amy told me that she was particularly confused about this because she had a wonderful relationship with both her father and mother. Her father was nurturing and adoring, and her mother had also been warm and loving toward Amy. Amy was under the impression that one needed to have an absent or bad father in order to develop such issues with men.

I noticed that the one thing Amy never mentioned during our conversations was what the relationship was like *between* her mother and father. When I pressed her on this issue, she revealed that her father had in fact treated her mother terribly. He was emotionally and verbally abusive, even going so far as to force her to walk a certain number of feet behind him whenever they were out in public. Amy, on the other hand, was allowed to walk beside him.

Because Amy was treated one way by her father but observed the opposite in the way he acted toward her mother, she created a script in which her value varied widely in different parts of her life. As her father was so encouraging of Amy growing up, she believed that she did have value when it came to her mind and intellectual pursuits, but she internalized the way her father treated her mother to mean that women had no value when it came to love. That is why a strong, successful woman like Amy allowed such abusive men into her life. Her love script told her that women should remain small and unimportant in the eyes of their men, and she attracted men who confirmed this belief.

Broken Love Script #2: *I Am Unworthy of Love*

I shared the fact that for many years I felt that I was unworthy of love because of the things that my mother, as well as my stepfather, told me as a child, but the same type of script can develop not only from what we are told but also from how we are treated.

Another client of mine, Mary, once told me all about her parents' wonderful marriage. Her mother and father clearly adored each other and presented a beautiful, healthy love model for Mary and her siblings to observe while they were growing up. Her parents were affectionate, loving, and kind to each other. They were also very successful and busy, and in their family the children's needs came last. Mary and her siblings were raised almost completely by hired help while their parents were busy traveling around the world, often away from them for many months at a time.

When Mary's parents came back from their trips, she and her

siblings often felt like a nuisance. It was clear to them that their parents would have preferred the freedom that came with life without children. As a result, Mary and her siblings idealized the idea of a marriage like their parents', but believed that they didn't deserve it. They internalized their parents' attitude toward them to mean that they were unlovable and undeserving of a healthy, loving marriage like the one their parents shared. Each of them took this on as their love script.

When I met Mary, she was attracting wonderful men who truly loved her, but she never trusted them and could never believe that they would ever really love her when her own parents did not. She would unknowingly sabotage each of her relationships, assuming that the men would end up leaving her. Eventually, they did. This is an incredibly common script that can be written in many different ways. The result is a feeling that we personally don't deserve love or a belief in the misconception that love is unattainable.

Broken Love Script #3: *Love Comes in the Form of Neglect or Abuse*

Those of us who grew up with abuse in our families often create a script that simply says abuse and love go hand in hand. You can't have one without the other, and we rarely learn to recognize love in any other form. But even people with healthy love role models can sometimes accept abuse as a part of love.

As you know, I grew up with two opposite role models when

it came to love and observed both ends of the love spectrum. My grandparents had a healthy and nurturing relationship and loved me in the same beautiful way. On the other side of the coin, I witnessed my mother attracting brutal, abusive men while I suffered emotional and physical abuse from her. From my grandparents, I learned that love could be healthy and pure, but I learned from my mother that love could also come in the form of severe neglect and abuse. This confused me on the very deepest level. On one hand, I knew what love could and should be, but I also bought into the lie that I could be neglected or abused in the name of love. As a result, my love script was split in two, and so I attracted men from both extremes.

In my rational mind, I knew that abuse had nothing to do with love, and I swore that I would never be with a man who abused me. But then I found myself in a relationship that I thought was modeled on my grandparents' healthy marriage until a man whom I was with slapped me across the face so hard that I flew off the chair I was sitting on. I didn't understand how I could have let this happen, and I struggled to reconcile the abuse in my mind. It sadly took two additional experiences with his physical abuse, including an encounter where I actually hit him, before I finally said, "Enough." Following these encounters, it took many years for me to realize that part of my love script told me that I could never have a relationship that was as healthy as my grandparents' because, for me, neglect and abuse were still a part of love.

Broken Love Script #4: *My Value Lies*
Only in My Beauty or Talent

Sometimes, being praised for the wrong thing—or merely one specific thing—can create identity issues and a love script that tells us that we're valued only for the wrong reasons. I often wondered how my mother, who was raised by wonderful and loving parents, attracted such abusive men as my stepfather, and it has taken me years to be able to analyze her own love script and find out the truth.

My grandmother became pregnant with my mother later in life (at the age of forty-two), and my mother was the beautiful, precious baby of the family. Life was good for my grandparents at that time. They loved each other, my grandfather was successful, and they had plenty of money, and now they had a cherished new little girl. Not only was she beautiful, but as you know, she was also very talented. When she was only three years old, they discovered that she had a lovely singing voice, and soon she was singing to our entire church congregation and even in radio jingles. She was like a little Shirley Temple quickly on her way to stardom.

My grandparents not only loved my mother, but my grandfather idolized her and loved nothing more than showing off his beautiful, talented little girl. When he had his business partners over to the house, especially during what was considered his late-night "happy hour," he would often wake her up and ask her to come downstairs and sing for them. My mother would end up entertaining these men into the wee hours of the night. My mother once told me that even though she knew her father had meant well and that he loved her, deep down she was hurt by this. She felt that all she had to offer in life was her looks and her singing voice, which was mostly what she received attention for, and never learned that her true value was really based on so much more.

This caused my mother to really struggle with her identity over the years, and ultimately to attract men who did not value her in the ways that she deserved. Her belief that her value lay solely in her beauty also caused my mother to become very critical of herself and others. Her script said that if someone (including herself) wasn't perfectly beautiful with a perfect body, then something was wrong with them. This belief system developed not from what she was told or even what she witnessed in her parents' marriage, but based on how she was treated as a young girl.

Broken Love Script #5: *No One Is Good Enough for Me*

A broken love script can sometimes create an overblown ego, but don't forget that oversize egos are just as damaged as small ones. In other words, someone who believes that others aren't good enough for them is just as broken as someone who thinks that they aren't good enough for others. Being hypercritical of one's self and others is one of the most common manifestations of a broken love script that I see in my clients, and a need for perfection can have many different root causes.

One of my clients, Sasha, was a straight-A student and a powerful athlete. As a girl, she could do no wrong. She was very proud of her accomplishments and of the attention that she received from her parents while growing up. Meanwhile, Sasha had a younger sister who was born with a learning disability. Her sister wasn't nearly as successful in school or as athletic as Sasha. Growing up, Sasha did not feel competitive with her sister, but her parents often compared the two girls, with Sasha always in the lead. It hurt Sasha deeply to see how these comparisons wounded her sister.

Once Sasha grew up and moved out on her own, the dynamic between her and her sister changed. She found herself becoming increasingly critical of her sister, wishing that she would just "get it together!" Soon these judgments extended to others. Sasha had trouble maintaining friendships with other women because she was so critical of them, and she continually rejected the men she met because she thought they weren't good enough for her. She could find something wrong with anybody, and it's true that nobody is perfect, but she considered these imperfections to be unacceptable.

When I met Sasha, the sweet, caring girl she had once been was desperately trying to get out. Sasha knew that her critical behavior had gotten out of control. In our work together, she realized that her parents' comparisons between her and her sister had caused her to harden herself because it pained her too much to see her sister put down in this way. The script she wrote said that one must be perfect in order to be lovable. It was her way of shutting out her sister's pain, and her compassion for her sister was turned inside out and instead became judgment and criticism. I worked with Sasha to put herself in her sister's shoes and to heal their relationship. This allowed her to rewrite her script, lighten up on her need for perfection, and become less critical of herself, her sister, and others around her.

Broken Love Script #6: *I Can Love Others Only by Rescuing or Parenting Them*

When a parent is stuck in his or her own way, it is very common for the child to develop a script that stars them as the caretaker whose only value is in nurturing or parenting the people in their life. In these cases, a parent either has an inappropriate lack of boundaries, low self-esteem, or simply never learned how to parent in a healthy way themselves. They look to their children to meet their unmet needs. These needs can range from emotional to physical, or even sexual. The broken love script that results in the child tells him or her that their purpose in a relationship is simply to meet the other person's needs.

One way this script can develop is if one spouse is busy or absent and the other spouse becomes lonely and starts to act out by having the child "fill in" for the missing partner, either emotionally (by becoming more of a companion for the parent than a child), physically (by cooking and cleaning and literally taking care of the parent), or even sexually (by being forced to fulfill a parent's sexual needs). These children simply don't ever have a chance to be children. They are forced to take care of their parents and then they grow up believing that love is based completely on their ability to nurture others. People with this script often find other broken people to rescue, because in their broken script they subconsciously believe that all they have to offer is their nurturing and care. If someone tries to love this person back or to nurture *them,* it is very uncomfortable for them to be the one being taken care of. In this way, they shut love out until they can rewrite their script to include other ways of loving and nurturing themselves.

Broken Love Script #7: *I Have No Value Outside a Relationship*

Too many people give all their power to the other person in their relationship. Sometimes this happens even before a relationship begins—when a woman tortures herself over whether or not a guy she met at a club will ever call or spends hours deciphering what a text message may have really meant. When you truly love yourself and believe in God's love for you, you don't have to worry about these things and would never give your power away to someone else, especially someone you hardly know.

It broke my heart when one of my clients, Annie, exhibited this broken script. She was a lovely woman in her sixties who hadn't dated in decades before I introduced her to a man. Although they liked each other, he felt that he wasn't ready to take the relationship any further, and broke it off after only a few months. I thought that Annie would be fine with this, as she had really been enjoying the experience of dating this man more than she really cared for him. But when I saw her soon after the breakup, I was shocked by her appearance! While before she had been youthful and vibrant and always taken care of herself, she now looked sad, disheveled, and much older. When I asked her what was going on, she claimed that she was depressed about the end of the relationship. It was terrible to see that she had given so much of her personal power to this brief relationship that she lost her vibrancy once it was over.

Although Annie wasn't one to go from relationship to relationship in need of validation, unfortunately too many people end up doing just that. They have a hard time being out of a relationship in fear of being unloved and alone. Annie and others with this script weren't loved enough or properly in their childhoods, and the result is a need for validation from others as an adult. All their power, value, and worth lies in how much another person likes them, and they need to heal from this so that they can love themselves and exhibit the same energy, passion, and vitality before, during, and after a relationship.

Reading Your Love Script

I hope that these examples have sparked some thoughts about your own love script and how it may have come to be written. It is time to uncover the hidden beliefs about yourself and about love so that you can open yourself up to true, life-changing love! Perhaps you feel that you already know exactly what is written in your love script, or maybe you believe that yours is already perfect as it is. Either way, there is more work to be done! I want to push you to really understand and accept every aspect of your love script so that you can rewrite it to become even more healthy and joyous.

If you think that you have no clue about what your love script has been telling you, I am confident that if you are completely honest with yourself, you will find that you already have the answers. In fact, the more you think about this, you will start to see that many different answers will come to you on many different levels. You must continue to peel back layers of your psyche to discover exactly how you ended up where you are today. Start by sitting quietly by yourself and thinking about everything you just read about love scripts. What rang true to you? Which stories reminded you either of your own life or the life of someone you know? Did you recognize yourself, your parents, or your siblings in any of these examples? As your thoughts start flowing, pull out your journal and write down everything that comes to mind, whether it's a story from your childhood, a memory about how your father treated your mother, or even a piece of dialogue straight out of your life's script.

Now let's take a look at what has worked well in your life so far and what has not. Where are you thriving? What parts of your life and pieces of your identity make you feel most comfortable? Next, think about which aspects of your life are not working as well as you would like. Write them down and then see if you can look back into your past once again and identify where this behavior may have come from. What beliefs are you holding on to that may be causing you to act in ways that aren't serving you well? For clues, think about how your parents treated each other, how they treated themselves, how each of them treated you, and what they said to you about your own worth and value.

Many of my clients balk when I say that it is their beliefs and their own actions that have been keeping them from experiencing the type of love they want, but you have so much more power than you realize. Your thoughts and actions created the parts of your life that both are and aren't working. It is so tempting to blame others for the problems in our lives, but this does not help us move forward. In fact, it keeps us plain stuck! It's up to you to identify what is wrong in your life, accept it, and then release it. This is the only way for things to change. In life, through ego and spirit, you attract and accept the things that you believe you deserve. Trust me—if something isn't working, there is a piece inside of you that truly believes that this is either as good as it's going to get or that it's all you really deserve. Your ego may not recognize this to be true, but your soul knows.

If someone is hurting you, they ultimately are not to blame. I know that this may sound harsh or insensitive, but I'm here to tell you the truth and to help you find your own truth, wisdom, and strength so that you are no longer a victim and can experience the love that is waiting. As long as you place the blame outside yourself, you lose your power. You are the one who has allowed the unhealthy relationships in and then kept them in your life. The first step is ask yourself why, but then you must push deeper to understand what it is about you that ever believed this was acceptable. Gently and respectfully ask yourself why you allowed this in your life to begin with. You must take ownership for your failures *and* successes so that you can ultimately get what you deserve. Things will never get better as long as you blame others for your circumstances.

Continue writing in your journal about what you think your love script might be telling you and where those beliefs came from. Keep going even if you don't think you know the answers, because deep down, you do. If you hit a roadblock or have a hard time coming up with any ideas about your own love script, it is likely that your ego has covered up the truth because it is too painful for you or your ego to deal with. It may be difficult, but you have to push through this pain in order to find the truth. Sometimes we hide the truth from ourselves because we are ashamed. Please don't blame yourself for taking a misstep or even for having followed a broken love script down a negative path. No one is judging you. It is not your fault, and you have done nothing wrong. God already forgives you, and now it is your turn to take a moment to forgive yourself. Only then will you be able to move forward in a more positive direction. Let's uncover this stuff, take a good look at it, and let it go. This is how you will grow, and how you will ultimately change your life for the better.

Rewriting Your Love Script

What you believe is what you create and attract in your life, and so you have already started to rewrite your love script simply by beginning the process of understanding your own areas of love sabotage and what has kept you from experiencing the love around you. In other words, by dispelling your previously subconscious negative beliefs about love, you have taken a huge step toward creating a healthy, loving relationship with yourself. This will ultimately lead you to find love with the right one!

Rewriting your love script is not something that you will be able to do overnight. It will happen over time as you become increasingly aware of your own true strengths as well as your areas of self-sabotage, where they came from, and how they are no longer serving you. As you move forward through the work in the book and as you walk through your daily life, try to become conscious of the moments when you find yourself "stuck in the script." This can happen when you are feeling stressed, insecure, or overwhelmed, and you suddenly realize that you are acting straight out of your broken love script. Catching yourself in these moments and correcting your thoughts and behavior to match your new beliefs about love will ultimately help you rewrite your script and attract the beautiful love that is all around you.

HOMEWORK ASSIGNMENT
Conduct a Love Survey

After taking some time to work on your love script, the following exercise can actually be really healing. I hope you will enjoy and learn from it.

This is quite an undertaking, but you will discover so much about yourself and others in the process! I am so excited for you to do this. Depending on your personality, the love survey can either be really fun and easy or quite a challenge, but either way it is very important that you do it.

To do this, take your journal with you to a few singles hot spots—they can be upscale lounges, neighborhood dives, or anything in between—perhaps even singles events at church. Approach five different men or women (the opposite sex). Let these people know that you are doing a survey about love and relationships as a piece of homework that you are working on, and that their answers are completely confidential. You don't even have to know their names! You are simply going to ask them four questions and write down their answers. Don't worry—in my many years of doing this with clients, not one of them has been turned down. However, if you happen to experience the first, that's okay; it means that there's something about love that they don't buy. Sad for them. The questions that you should ask them are as follows:

1. Do you believe in love?
2. What does love mean to you?
3. If you could have the perfect love, what would it look like?
4. How well were you truly loved growing up?

The purpose of this assignment is to illustrate that we all really want the same things. Men and women alike want to be loved and to know that love is real. These questions will get you on the same level and show you that strangers of the opposite sex aren't as different or scary as you may think.

When you're finished, go home and write down your own answers to these questions. It's important that you do this after conducting the survey because I want you to think about whether your answers are the same then as they would have been before doing the survey or if they have shifted. If they have shifted, why? What do you think the survey has taught you?

FIVE-DAY LOVE REALITY CHECK

Now that you have completed your self-appraisal and spent some time thinking about your own love script, you are developing a true awareness of what love is and are beginning to sense it all around you. Things should be clicking into place in your mind, clearly telling you where you've been stuck in the past and why. This is the time to get excited about finally *getting out of your own way* and moving forward to experience the fullness of love that God has waiting for you right around the corner!

DAYS 11–15

CHAPTER SIX
Love Role Models

A S I HAVE mentioned, your love role models are the examples of love and marriage that you observed while you were growing up. These include your parents, grandparents, aunts and uncles, friends' parents, and any other adults who were part of your life. The way they treated each other and talked to each other, the way they showed affection for each other, and even the ways that they argued or fought all played a role in creating your love script and all your ideas about love and marriage, even if you don't agree with them.

If you happen to be someone who came from a loving set of parents who loved you deeply in return, you are not only fortunate but, sadly, more of an anomaly than you may know.

Unfortunately, too many people grow up with negative love role models—divorced or unhappily married parents, abusive relationships, or lonely single parents who told us that love was cruel, painful, or just plain unnecessary. The experience of growing up with these negative role models is one of the biggest reasons that so many of my clients have stopped believing in love. They didn't see it growing up, and they can't find it now, so it must all be pointless—or so they think. Don't forget that we create what we believe, and so, if you don't believe in love, you will never be able to experience love. Your fears will be confirmed because you will not be open to giving and receiving love and you will be unable to recognize it around you.

Even as adults, we are surrounded by negative role models in the media, which perpetuate our brokenness and continue to keep us from love. Think about the marriages that we read about in the tabloids and the images of love and relationships that we see on reality TV. These are almost unanimously negative representations of love, and they have a much greater impact on our psyches than most of us realize. We may allow ourselves to be entertained by the ridiculous or sad breakups that we read about in magazines, but these stories continually tell us that there is no such thing as a real relationship or marriage. They remind us over and over that love is always fleeting and that all marriages—even if they seem perfect—are actually about to fall apart. Our subconscious minds take on this belief, and as a result we begin to lose faith in and trivialize love. Overly romantic images of love actually serve as equally negative role models. In a show like *The*

Bachelor, helicopter rides to exotic settings, unrealistically beautiful surroundings, and constant excitement work together to create expectations that are almost impossible to maintain over the long term when it comes to love, if the foundation for authentic love hasn't been set first. This can be extremely damaging, and sets up both the "contestants" on the show and the viewers at home to fail.

If our experiences with love at home were ugly, we pick up a magazine and see breakups being celebrated on every page, and then we turn on the TV and see an impossibly beautiful couple being draped in luxury and nearly drowned in champagne all in the name of love, and we become bombarded by negativity, again without even realizing it. The result is a real brokenness around the very idea of love, along with a *dumbing down* of our value systems, our behaviors, and our actions when it comes to love. Ultimately, we start to believe that love does not really exist. What we see in the world feels so out of control that it leads many of us to turn to addiction and other self-destructive behaviors just to numb out and feel good, when instead what we really want is love. We cannot imagine how to even love ourselves in the midst of all this brokenness. As children, we are told fairy tales in which everyone lives "happily ever after," but then what we see around us makes us think that this was a lie. I want you to know that this is wrong. The real lie is that love doesn't exist and that there is no such thing as happily ever after. I believe that your happily ever after *is* out there waiting for you! I'm living proof and so are the *hundreds* of happily married clients I've matched.

Your New Love Role Model

If you want to find love, you must first believe in it. Trust me when I say that I understand how hard it can be to believe in love if you did not witness it growing up. As you know, I did have wonderful love role models in my grandparents, but again, my mother unfortunately presented a very negative model that I believed was an equally important part of love. Most of us didn't have role models that were either completely positive or 100 percent negative, but the negativity that we saw was enough to taint our idea of love, and the heartaches that we experience in our own lives confirm these negative beliefs.

In order to create new love role models for yourself, I want you to grasp on to the healthy images of love that you did witness. Even if your parents' relationship was horrendous, you must have caught a glimpse of real love between other family members or even a friend's parents. Think back to what you witnessed in that relationship and how it made you feel. Perhaps the only image of healthy love that you observed as a child was a couple at the grocery store, laughing together and holding hands. Even if you feel that you witnessed love and partnership between a couple only once, that still means that your soul carried that memory for a reason. Go back to a time when you saw something that felt good and pure—something that looked like real love. What couples did you look at as a child and think, "I want to have that one day"? Hold on to those moments and write them down in order to keep them fresh and alive in your mind. Those relationships are your true love role models, and surrounding yourself with these people and memories will remind you that love does exist and what it really looks like.

If you can't think of a single healthy image of love that you witnessed growing up, I want to first commend you for continuing to believe in love, anyway. You may feel like you've given up, but if you had truly given up on love, you wouldn't have picked up this book. Just by reading these words, you are calling love closer to you by thinking about love and putting out loving energy. You can be *your own* love role model by showing your faith in love. I not only want you to know that love exists, I want you to be able to picture exactly what it looks like for you and what your heart tells you it should look like. If you feel that you have had no positive love role models to grasp on to and want a love role model other than yourself, I will share stories from my clients' happy marriages as well as my own. Trust in my descriptions of these real but beautifully *imperfect* relationships of love, and know that God has the same thing waiting for you, as God's love for us is perfect.

Lance and I have been together for more than fifteen years and married for almost twelve. What is the best part of our marriage? I would say it is our genuine friendship, the camaraderie and freedom that come with knowing that we always have each other's back. We have a true best friendship, and we can laugh together and act silly together without any fear of judgment. Lance and I are always seeking to learn together. We passionately pray together and share our faith and love of God with each other, even though he is Jewish and I am Christian. I am still *incredibly* attracted to him and we share a fabulous sex life to this day. Is it always like this? Of course not. There are days when one of us wakes up on the wrong side of the bed to put it mildly, and during stressful times, we both have to fight hard to avoid reverting to the broken love scripts that we learned growing up. And we each have idiosyncrasies that can drive the other crazy.

Yes, sometimes we fight. Real love is not always free of conflict! But perhaps the most beautiful thing about our marriage is how far we've come together. We've grown up, and we are still growing! If you are familiar with the "ego states" of psychology (adult, parent, child), we were each in our wounded "child" ego state in the beginning of our marriage. During an argument ten years ago, there were probably some f-bombs thrown on each end, we might have slammed doors, and we were known to give each other the silent treatment for days. Now we know how to give each other space. When an argument arises, we take a healthy and mutual time-out, regroup, and look within for the cause. We avoid letting things escalate this way, and almost always get back together and say, "Sorry, baby, let's try this communication thing again," or, "That wasn't your fault. I was just really stressed and in a bad mood."

In any relationship, you need to be able to set your ego aside in order to see where your anger truly comes from and to understand your own actions. Lance and I both have weaknesses, but as a result of the work we've done together and within ourselves, we can talk about them and be honest with each other. So many couples fall in love but then become enemies instead of allies as soon as things get tough. This is most often because their egos don't allow them to be honest with themselves or each other about what is really going on. This is why it is so important to fully love yourself before finding love with someone else!

As I said, as wonderful as my marriage is to Lance, it is not perfect, and I want to be completely honest with you about how imperfect it can be. The truth is that there was a time even when writing this book when I realized that our marriage, "we," needed more healing and change. I came to this realization after filming *Lovetown, USA,* where I was able to spend a lot of time by myself listening to my inner voice and honoring my feelings, something that had been lost amid running a business and a home while being a mom, wife, sister, and friend. This process helped me feel stronger and more confident than I had ever felt before, and when it was time to wrap up filming and return home, I realized that I didn't want to leave. I felt like I would lose a part of myself by going home, and I had to do the difficult work of looking at myself, my life, and my marriage to find out what was making me feel this way.

I realized that I often felt silenced in my marriage and that this needed to change. In truth, this is something that I probably should have been aware of sooner, but again, I got caught up in the busyness of life (as so many people do) and had been shutting out my inner voice. When we abandon that inner voice, we cannot experience the wholeness of love, and I needed to reconnect to myself in order to heal my marriage. Luckily, I was able to find my voice again, and Lance and I grew even stronger by addressing this issue and working through it together.

If you are unable to grasp on to a healthy image of love that you witnessed as a child, it is unlikely that you were able to see what happened in this relationship during the tough times that come along in any marriage. Witnessing tenderness and affection will help convince you that love is real, but you need a more fleshed-out model of real love in order to understand the true depth and complexities of love and marriage. I want to paint an accurate picture for you of what a healthy marriage really looks like in the best and worst of times, in case you weren't able to witness this growing up. No matter where you are today on your journey to finding love, reading these examples of how conflict can be handled in a healthy way will flesh out your new, positive love role models.

Money

Most people know that money is a major cause of conflict in many marriages, but why is this the case? What makes finances such a sensitive topic for so many of us? Your relationship with money is based on what you were taught as a child, and therefore we all have different attitudes about how to properly earn, save, and spend money! Our ideas about money are tightly connected to our egos, many times making it very difficult to compromise, communicate, and learn from a partner about money.

A client of mine named Sarah grew up without any healthy

example of how to respect and value money. Her parents were both born into wealthy families and never had to earn their own money. All Sarah knew about money growing up was that if you wanted something, you went out and bought it. There was no work ethic modeled for her at home, and Sarah never learned how to be responsible with money. When she grew up and started to earn her own money as a successful lawyer, she continued this trend by spending money as soon as she earned it with no thought of the true value of money. Despite the fact that she was very successful, Sarah ended up living paycheck to paycheck, because she never understood the importance of saving and investing her money.

In her first marriage, money was a constant source of conflict between Sarah and her husband, Bill. Bill had a very different experience with money as a child. His parents owned their own company and were doing well throughout his childhood, but when he was a teenager they lost everything. This taught Bill how to respect money without ever taking it for granted, and he was very cautious with the money he earned. Sarah and Bill constantly fought about money, because neither of them understood or respected how the other came to treat money.

Unfortunately, the marriage did not last, and when Sarah came to me she still blamed Bill for being so critical of her spending habits. We worked together to uncover the truth about where Sarah's ways with money came from and as she came to know her authentic self, her ego about her spending habits cooled off. She was then able to enter a new relationship where she could be open to learning and compromising about a different way to handle finances. Her second husband, Grant, was also a saver, but this time Sarah appreciated this about him instead of resenting it. She knew that without his savings, they wouldn't have been able to afford the beautiful house they bought or many of the nice things they shared. Sarah was able to surrender to herself and the pieces of her that were holding her back when it came to finances. She opened up her soul and spirit to learning a better way. Her spending style and Grant's are still different, but they have learned from each other and found a compromise that works. Sarah now understands the importance of savings, so she always puts a portion of her earnings in savings and some toward the household expenses first. Then she can use a portion of the remainder to reward herself for her hard work! When you have a healthy ego, you can learn from the other person, find genuine compromise, and in this way not just avoid unnecessary fights but build a lasting and true sense of partnership.

Faith

Even those of us who have a strong relationship with God don't always realize how important a role faith plays in our relationships. I believe that it is essential to share beliefs about religion with your spouse. When things get tough or downright frightening in marriage, you need to have something bigger than both of you that you can turn to. This does not mean that you and your spouse need to share the exact same religious background, although it can make things easier in many ways. It is a shared *faith* in something higher than yourselves that will strengthen a marriage, not necessarily shared religion.

As you already know, I am very strong in my faith and my relationship with God is very important to me. Growing up, the only thing I learned about Jewish people was that they didn't believe in Jesus. Knowing very little if anything about Jews made me sad for their loss of what I believed was a true and personal relationship with God. When I became born again, I knew that I could never be with someone who didn't believe in Jesus, and I turned down every Jewish man who was willing to take a chance on me. I thought that if we didn't both know Jesus, then we didn't both know God. Yet somehow, when I met Lance, I didn't care about his religion because we instantly had such a strong spiritual connection that was beyond anything I had experienced with the most *Christian* of men. When we finally talked about his Jewish faith and I had the opportunity to experience it firsthand with his family, I fell in love with Judaism and realized on a deep spiritual level that my faith was born from his faith. Seeking to understand more about Lance's faith helped me understand my own even more. Lance felt the same way about me. Our relationship has brought each of us closer to God, and God has brought each of us closer together.

Sex

Sex is another area where our egos can get involved and make us feel insecure, resentful, or even complacent. These negative feelings can of course lead to a major disconnection and to some pretty negative fights. I do not believe that sex is the foundation of a marriage. It does not create the marriage or even keep it together. Love, respect, friendship, and camaraderie are the true building blocks of marriage, and these things should always come before sex. However, making love in a marriage is important! This is how we consummate our marriages and completely unite our body and soul with our partner's. Sex exists not only for procreation but to keep us strongly connected. Every time we make love, we secrete chemicals that keep us bonded together. This is why it is so important to continue making love throughout a marriage, not only for our marriage's spiritual health but for our mental and physical health, as well! And it can be just plain fun!

Marital fights about sex occur most often when we've lost our emotional intimacy, our connection to each other, and we become complacent and sex starts to feel like a chore. One spouse may become resentful if they feel that they must make love even when they don't feel like it. In other cases, a partner may get angry if they are not having sex as often as they would like. It's hard not to become complacent about sex when life gets busy and to take your partner for granted even if you and your spouse previously shared a wonderful sex life. In these cases, it is crucial that you find a way to reconnect on the issues that have created this disconnect. Start gently with a conversation that is honest and *nonshaming,* followed by soothing, *nonsexual* touching that will in turn restimulate the senses and remind each other not only of why you fell in love in the first place but of the great lovemaking that you can once again have! Try to remember how it felt when you first kissed or the first time you made love! Those feelings don't have to go away, and if you had them once, you will have them again.

Ruts do happen, and they don't mean that a marriage is over or even necessarily in trouble. A rut is simply a reminder of the importance to reconnect with your spouse. One of my girlfriends, Andrea, recently told me about a rut she got into with her husband, Tom. Andrea and Tom are both teachers and they had two young children of their own at home. They simply became too busy. Before they knew it, weeks, then months had gone by without them having sex. At first, Andrea was worried that her marriage was doomed, but one day Tom called her at work during lunchtime and said in a sexy tone, "I really need to see you; come home right now." They had never met in the middle of the day like that before!

As Andrea raced home, she felt nervous butterflies in her stomach. The excitement that she had experienced in the beginning of her marriage to Tom suddenly returned. When they made love, it was as fabulous as it ever had been and the rut between them was over. Resentment and fights about sex can happen when we buy into the lie that the way things are today is the way they will always be. Andrea and Tom avoided this by reminding each other how great their lovemaking could be. Marriage is constantly changing and evolving, and so is lovemaking within a marriage. It is up to *each* partner to work together to keep their sex life the way they want it to be!

Parenting

Many couples are happy and excited to start a family, but realize as the kids grow up that they have very different attitudes about how to discipline their children. This is something that couples absolutely need to talk about before getting married, but too many people fail to think it through at all. How you were parented as a child is in many ways exactly how you will parent your own children unless you pay attention and think about the things you want to do differently. If your ego is still wounded from the way you were disciplined as a child, you will be likely to not only discipline your children in the same way but become defensive about your own discipline style, making it difficult for you and your partner to come to a place of healthier parenting. When you get defensive, it means that your psyche already knows you are in the wrong, but your ego is covering up that truth. This can obviously lead to miscommunication and unnecessary fights between spouses.

My grandparents were completely nonshaming and noncritical of me when I was a child, but as you know, my mother was the exact opposite. Luckily, I couldn't just mindlessly follow the pattern I had experienced growing up, and had to choose between the vastly different parenting styles. I made a conscious decision about how I wanted to parent my sons. Lance's parents were of a different parenting style, one that, as he has shared, came with a lot of criticism and shame toward him as a child. This wasn't healthy or supportive of his self-esteem, and I'm happy to say that

Lance's parents have learned from this and act differently today. Lance and I agreed early on that we wanted to be noncritical parents, but I noticed that he tended to revert to his parents' shaming parenting style whenever he was feeling stressed. When this happened, I would remind him to listen to his tone and change the way he was talking to the kids.

When this happened five or ten years ago, Lance would say, "Don't tell me what to do" or "There's nothing wrong with my tone," dismissing me just as his feelings were often dismissed as a child. This would trigger my own childhood wounds from my mother and lead to huge fights between us. Over the years, we have each been able to look at the things that were holding us back and heal ourselves from our own past wounds. This has made our marriage so much stronger and more mature. A few years ago, we had a major blowout and after we made up, Lance said to me, "I am so sick of fighting with you. Let's make a pact that you have the right to call me out, and when you do I will trust that you are doing it because you care."

Now if I gently tell Lance to change his tone with the kids, he will thank me for reminding him instead of becoming defensive. We both trust that we are calling each other to a higher self rather than trying to "win." We do this for each other so we can grow and become better people and better parents. To this day, when he sees me go to a place of ugliness, Lance asks me, "What's going on right now?" Because I know that he's asking from a place of love, I can look inside myself and discover what is really going on.

It was not always like this, but we got here by getting our

egos out of the way and really seeing each other with a love and awareness of how we each came to be the way we are. Before we were able to do this, our egos stepped up front and center and we blamed the other person for *every* problem that arose, instead of looking within. This behavior put up walls between us that made us blind and deaf to each other and kept love out. By compassionately understanding each other, Lance and I have been able to tear down those walls, break away from our egos, and grow together in love. Although some of you might be married and see a piece of yourself in this or learn from what I've shared, I especially have in mind those of you who are waiting for marriage to knock on your door. You can see what wonderful things you have coming and be prepared for what can be very normal and in need of some healing, with the faith that the full experience of love will include healthy conflict, joy, and growth.

HOMEWORK ASSIGNMENT
Open Your Eyes to Love

As you begin opening your mind to the idea that love exists all around you, I want you to begin opening your heart to the fact that your soul mate is out there waiting for you. Although you have no idea where or when you will find him or her, each time you put this book down and go out into the world and interact with people, I want you to look into everyone's eyes while holding on to the possibility that he or she could be the one! Simply reminding yourself of this potential and really challenging yourself to be open to love will make you feel giddy and excited about love's possibilities. This will shift your energy, attract others to you, and bring love closer and closer. As you do this, take some time to think about the love role models in your own life. Now, pull out your journal and write down all the positive images of love that you've seen and wish to emulate.

CHAPTER SEVEN
Love Gone Wrong

I AM CONSTANTLY SURPRISED and saddened to find that the vast majority of people who come into my office hoping to find love are actually scared to death of love because of past relationships that went wrong. They say to me, "I know that love exists, and I've seen it and experienced it, but I will never truly open my heart to love again." Many of these people think that this attitude cannot stop them from falling in love again, and that a new love might heal their wounds, but their fear is actually an enormous roadblock when it comes to experiencing love. It is the very thing that is keeping them from meeting the person who is out there waiting for them right now. Yes, your own soul mate is out there waiting for you, too, but you won't be able to meet him or her until you can love yourself, know yourself, and understand your part in each of your failed relationships so that you can truly heal.

Maybe you're wondering how true love can go wrong when I already said that love can never hurt you. Well, it was not the love in a failed relationship that hurt you. It was your ego and your partner's ego, and bad decisions on both your parts. In fact, had you healed and come to better know yourself before entering the relationship, it might have ended quite differently. That's not to say that you missed out on being with "the one"! We never miss the opportunity to be with our soul mates, because I believe that God does not allow us to meet them until we are truly ready.

I can't tell you how many men and women come to me and say, "I let the right one go!" It's an especially common story that I hear from men who cheated on or left a wonderful woman as long as twenty or thirty years ago and now deeply regret it. Many of these men are married now and still blame themselves for letting their "soul mates" slip through their fingers, but it is impossible that these women were actually their soul mates. First of all, if they were cheating or otherwise behaving badly, these men clearly weren't ready back then to find their soul mates. I also believe that these men let these women go for a reason deeper than they were aware of. They must learn to trust themselves, trust in God's plan, and forgive themselves.

If you, too, are still mourning a lost love, you must forgive yourself so that you can move on to find your true soul mate. That person you let go was not the right one for you, and it wasn't God's timing, or else you wouldn't have let him or her go. It's as simple as that. Trust that God was speaking to you when you said or did something to end that relationship, and know that you are on the right path now. In order to move on and find real love, you need to heal from past relationships rather than yearn for them. We don't want to be afraid or judgmental of what we experienced but to be aware and learn from it.

Maybe you have been wounded by another person's actions or behaviors in a relationship. Perhaps you were neglected, abused, or cheated on, and you need to heal from that pain before you can move on. It may surprise you, but the steps that you need to take in order to heal are exactly the same if you were the victim or the perpetrator, the abuser or the abused. In order to move on from love gone wrong, you need to recognize your love teachers (more on this below), be honest about your own role in the relationship's demise, allow love to penetrate and heal you, look back with compassion and understanding, and trust in God. I'll share more details about some of my clients' and my own past love traumas as I guide you through each of these steps toward healing.

Recognize Love Teachers in Each Past Relationship

Our *love teachers* are the people in our lives with whom we experience the feelings of love but who aren't our soul mates. Regardless of how each past relationship has ended or, more important, what it included, know that *each* relationship we enter shows us who we *truly* are, what we have left to heal, and how *lovable* we are. Our love teachers serve as *mirrors* that reflect a different view of who we are, and where we are with our healing and love readiness. We are not meant to marry these people, but we can have brilliant learning experiences with them. Unfortunately, many people settle too soon out of fear and spend the rest of their lives feeling like they missed out on meeting their true soul mates. The result is an okay relationship instead of an amazing deep relationship.

I recently ran into an old friend who said, "Kailen, I know you're a relationship expert and so I need to ask you a question." He went on to tell me how much he loves his wife, how beautiful he thinks she is, what a good mother she is, and that they share a great sex life. He said that he would never cheat on her because he truly loves and respects her, but he believes in his heart that she isn't his soul mate. He couldn't explain why, but he simply feels like something is missing. The truth is that he's probably right. His wife most likely isn't his true soul mate. She was probably meant to be one of his love teachers, but they ended up marrying each other instead. Of course, they can still share a beautiful marriage, but although this may sound harsh, I believe they would have been happier if they had recognized that they were *love teachers* before committing to each other so that *each* of them had the chance to find their *true* soul mate.

To illustrate how recognizing your love teachers can help you heal from a past love, let me tell you about a client of mine named Carmen, who fell in love with David when they were in high school. He was her first love, her first lover, and every first for her.

She loved his parents and became a part of his family. Carmen and David were very much in love, and there wasn't one thing that she didn't love and adore about him. Luckily enough, he felt the same way about her.

When they graduated from high school, David and Carmen went off to opposite ends of the country. With David in college in Los Angeles and Carmen working as a waitress in New York, they maintained a long-distance relationship and planned to get engaged one day. But as Carmen began to experience more of the world, she became tempted by other men and one night after *too* much to drink, she ended up betraying David. When she told David the truth about what had happened, he was devastated and broke up with her. Carmen didn't blame David for leaving her, but she was heartbroken after their breakup, and greatly regretted her actions. When she came to me more than twenty years later, Carmen still blamed herself for making the biggest mistake of her life and believed that she would never again find love like she had shared with David.

I worked with Carmen to discover everything that she learned from her relationship with David, and she was ultimately able to realize David's role in her life as a *love teacher*. She can now look back happily on how much they loved each other and how precious their first experience of love with a partner was. By coming to terms with the end of their relationship, Carmen also realized how grateful she should be that she and David aren't still together! As a young woman, there was simply more that she needed to see and learn and experience. She was right to follow this instinct, but of course she should have done it in a more honest way by telling David that she was feeling tempted rather than cheating, and needed to start dating other people.

Healing from her relationship with David allowed Carmen to open herself up to experiencing new love with another man. Not long after, she ended up falling madly in love with her soul mate! If you have been desperately holding on to a past love because you regret letting that person go, begin to heal by thinking about what you learned from that person. What did he or she teach you about love, relationships, and family? What did you teach them? Was there a voice inside you saying that you needed to move on or experience something different? You need to trust in yourself and in God and know that you could never have really missed out on your soul mate. When you connect to your soul mate, it's a passionate decision in one's soul that commits you to the other, to love, healing, and growth. The person you let go was not that person. He or she was simply a love teacher, and recognizing their role in your life is the first step toward healing.

Be Honest about Your Role in the Relationship's Demise

We must learn from each of our failed relationships so that we can be healthier and happier in the next one. Some of my clients claim that the end of their relationship was completely their partner's fault and they did absolutely nothing wrong themselves. Clearly, these people are stuck in a place of ego and cannot see the truth about their own actions, but hiding from the truth about their own responsibility will only keep them stuck. You must be accountable for your own behavior in every failed relationship so that you can forgive yourself and move on to experience the love that God has waiting.

Even in the most extreme examples—if you were cheated on or abused—you played a role by allowing this person into your life in the first place. Don't get me wrong—I'm not saying that it's your fault if someone has abused you, but you must see that you've played a role in what and whom you've accepted into your life. Because of an unhealed wound, you've ignored red flags and haven't listened to your inner voice.

I speak from experience about this. After separating from my first husband, I wasn't looking for another relationship, but when I met a wonderful young man, I was moved by his incredible kind and positive energy, the way he treated people, and especially his relationship with his family. Although I wasn't yet officially divorced, I found myself falling in love with him. For two years, we enjoyed a wonderful relationship, an almost perfect one, actually. I truly believed that he was my soul mate because of this.

Throughout my relationship with him, I found myself healing from the wounds of my childhood. I was turning into a joyful being that I never knew existed. But one day, he told me that he had been having a relationship with another man the entire time that he had been with me.

At that moment, I felt that everything I had experienced as love was a lie, and I became very hardened. He promised to get help and begged me to stay, but I was too angry. For years, I held on to my anger at him for betraying me, but after being honest with myself about my own role in this, I have finally been able to move forward. The truth is that I had no business being in a relationship with him at that time. I wasn't even divorced from my first husband yet! His lie to me was that he was faithful, but my lie to him and to myself was that I was fully available. A lie begets a lie. I now realize that my entire relationship with him could have gone differently if I had been more honest with him and finished the work I needed to do in my marriage before getting involved with him. Meanwhile, he should have done his own work and been honest about who he really was before getting involved with me. But it is by accepting my own role and my own responsibility rather than blaming others that has helped me to heal and grow.

Look Back with Compassion and Understanding

Once you've forgiven yourself for your own behavior that may have contributed to the end of a relationship, you must go back and forgive the other person for theirs. This doesn't mean that you have to condone every one of their actions. It simply means that you understand the level of brokenness that person was dealing with and accept that it was their brokenness that caused them to act this way. You must forgive them on a deep, spiritual level so that you can take the good from that relationship and move on with a healthy, clean, open slate to find your real partner.

My dramatic relationship with the last man I mentioned is a good example of this, too. After he told me about his affair, he revealed that he had been touched inappropriately by an adult when he was a young boy, and it had left scars. Of course for a long time I was angry with him for betraying me, but by seeking *with love* to understand the truth about what led him to act this way, I have been able to forgive him. Do I wish that he had been faithful to me? Of course, but I wouldn't trade the relationship that we shared for anything in the world, and I am not angry at him one speck today. It can be difficult, but in order to heal from a past wound, you must seek to find the truth with compassion and understanding. This person did not hurt you simply because they are a bad person. He or she is suffering and broken somewhere deep inside, and only knows how to act this one way in a love relationship. You do not have to applaud their behavior, but I do advise you to forgive them and let go of anger so that you can move forward to experience true love.

Allow Love to Penetrate and Heal

I have seen many of my clients attempt to move on from a failed relationship by jumping right into another one. This is an extremely common way of keeping yourself in the dark by busying yourself with relationship after relationship. Of course, this never works. A man or woman cannot heal you, but love itself can heal you if you allow it to penetrate your soul. As I said, when I fell in love with the man after my first husband, he loved me so intensely and so beautifully that it felt as if I was beginning to heal from the many wounds of my childhood. I later realized that he wasn't what was healing me. It was the things that I learned from our relationship, primarily the fact that I was lovable and fully capable of giving and receiving love. This helped me begin to write a new love script for myself.

Sending love to a former partner instead of hate or resentment can also help heal your own wounds from that relationship. I'll use Jessica, a client of mine, as an example. Unfortunately, shortly after Jessica was diagnosed with cancer, her long-term boyfriend left her and immediately began a relationship with another woman. Jessica responded with a combination of hatred and resentment while also blaming herself for the breakup. She was torn between hating this man and wanting him back, and I worked with Jessica to fully experience each of these feelings so that she could move forward from them.

I told Jessica to send her ex love instead of anger and resentment. If he wasn't the guy that she was meant to be with at that moment, then he wasn't her guy. She needed to trust this, and actually thank him for letting her go, so that she could find and be with the man God had waiting. Holding on to negative emotions, no matter how justified, was harmful to her spirit and her body. Sending love instead of anger sends a gentle release of anxiety, which brings peace within. By choosing to send love instead of hatred, you alter the chemicals in your brain and shift your emotions from a place of anxiety and fear, to a place of love and peace. The last thing Jessica needed at that time was to be holding on to such negative and harmful emotions, and I taught her how allowing love in and *out* can heal your mind and heal your body.

Trust in God

After the end of each relationship I've been in, especially those that were painful, I asked God why he would allow me to suffer such heartbreak. But in the end, I always trusted in his plan for me and knew that I would one day find my soul mate. The same is true for you. God, through granting free will, will continue to allow the wrong people to enter your life until you are seeking love with 100 percent truth and a loving, authentic self. If there is anything less, God will not stand in your way, because he wants you to learn. Not until you have done the work and healed yourself will you be able to fully experience true love.

But trust in God can also help you heal. After my relationship with this last man, I was completely closed off. I met a man who was funny and gorgeous, but I wasn't attracted to him, I wasn't ready. He kept pursuing me, but I continually turned him down. I simply wasn't open to accepting someone's love. I was willing to become friends though, and we ended up spending a lot of time together in a very platonic friendship. This all changed the day I met his mother. She was one of the most verbally abusive women I had ever experienced, and witnessing the way she treated this man softened my heart toward him. My heart broke for him, and I, being a well-trained caretaker from childhood and quite co-dependent at the time, allowed myself to fall in love with him so that I could "protect" him. I was happy to take care of his heart, but I could never truly allow him to have mine. Although I had done some healing from my past relationship, I was clearly in no place to enter into another, for I was unknowingly still quite toxic.

After dating this man for almost two years, I became pregnant, and he ended up becoming my second son's father. I wanted to do the right thing, and so did he, and so we got engaged—well, "promised." Earlier in the book, I told you a little bit about how I was getting more and more involved with my clients at this time and that hearing about them meeting their soul mates made me think twice about my own relationship. Although this man and I had now been together for many years, shared a son, and did learn and grow to truly love each other the best we knew how, there was always something very deep missing between us that sadly couldn't be denied.

Then one day, God spoke to me and said, *"This is not the man that you're supposed to be with. You have to trust Me. You will find love again."* As much as I knew what I was hearing was true, it was very difficult for me to take another son from his father and end a relationship of many years that (while not perfect) did have lovely times and deep friendship. I got down on my knees and prayed. I said, "I believe You. Although scared, I'm ready. Show me the way."

As I mentioned early on in this book, I knew that to find *the kind of* love that my clients had, I was the one who had to do the work and do it right this time. I *finally* got out of my and God's way and trusted that God would bring him to me. You know that it was then that I ended my relationship with my second son's father, telling him that I loved him but I knew we weren't soul mates. By trusting God and his plan for me, I was able to move on from that relationship with an open heart and ultimately find my own soul mate in Lance, and he was able to finally meet his. We are all friends until this day. I'm not repeating myself to be redundant; sometimes it takes hearing something this important a few times before we truly start to let the truth within the message stick! At least, it took me that long!

HOMEWORK ASSIGNMENT

Who Are You?

Open your journal and begin to write the answer to the question "Who am I?" After you're finished, think about how accurate a picture you've portrayed of yourself, and then write another version. Then do this again so that in the end you have three full answers. You may find that you would have answered this question differently at the beginning of this book! This is something that I will ask all my clients to do time and time again, until they connect in a way that brings a smile to their heart and their soul! We sometimes have to do this over and over again before we begin to get at the truth—the way God sees us! Since I'm not there with you to push you, you must hold yourself accountable or ask a trusted friend to read your answer and tell you if you've been honest. Deep down, we all know who we are, but this truth is often hidden from us. Revealing it will help you align your thoughts, actions, and even the way you look with your true spirit and personality, and it is then that love's full experience can come in.

FIVE-DAY LOVE REALITY CHECK

After embracing new love role models and learning the truth about your past relationships that may have failed, you might go through a brief stage of mourning at this point. This is okay, as it is necessary to mourn the times you have gotten in your own way in the past so that you can get out of your way and undergo what I like to call your Love Metamorphosis! So embrace what you've learned, let go of shame, and enjoy where you are now! You have been working hard and you deserve it! As you shed your old skin, allow the trust, awareness, and joy waiting underneath to take over and guide you onward. Be patient with yourself as you experience a mix of emotions, forgive the person you used to be, and you'll continue to move closer than ever to becoming the *real* you and experiencing real love! I know this process can be deep and at times intense, but trust me, it's worth it. After all the reading and learning, you'll enjoy what's to come even more!

DAYS 16–20

CHAPTER EIGHT

Love Design

D O YOU FEEL yourself coming closer to your true, authentic self? Would you say that you possibly feel more *you* than ever before?! If you have honestly done all the work in the book thus far, you should feel yourself blossoming as you transform into the true self that has been hiding inside you. I hope that you are enjoying an increased confidence and a new relationship with yourself! I also hope that by working so hard on understanding and healing yourself, you now appreciate the importance of truly loving yourself, away from your ego, before you can even try to experience love with someone else. Now that you are able to honor your true self, we can move on to focus on dating, relationships, and how to navigate and assess them in order to find your true soul mate. We'll start by determining the type of people you have been attracting into your life thus far, and then I will help you figure out what you should really be prioritizing in a potential partner based on your true wants and needs.

Love Shopping

One of my favorite (and by far one of the most eye-opening) exercises that I do with my clients is to take them love shopping. Through twenty years of trial and error with my clients, I have learned that there is much more going on than meets the eye when it comes to who we are attracted to and why. I realized that as people become closer to knowing their true selves, they naturally hone their ability to be attracted to the right partner for them. Then as their energy shifts and they transform into their authentic selves, they also begin to attract the right partner to them. Love shopping is an important step in determining who your soul and spirit are really attracted to by putting your ego's preferences aside.

If you're feeling brave enough, I suggest that you do this exercise by yourself. If you feel like you need to have someone with you, it's extremely important that you bring the right person. If the accountability partner who helped you with the blueprint was honest and authentic with you, that person would be a good choice. Be sure not to bring anyone who might steer you back toward the kinds of people you used to be attracted to, or who will encourage you to indulge in any unhealthy behaviors. This person must be dedicated to helping you discover your true self and equally committed to helping you find true love.

Once you decide whether to go love shopping alone or with someone else, you need to find the right time and place for this exercise. It is best to go somewhere that will be very busy and full of people of the opposite sex in the age group that you're interested in dating. There should be a variety of people there, too, not just a large group of people who are all very similar. It can be anywhere—a club, a bar, a restaurant, a gym, a sports event, church, or even Grand Central Terminal. Grab your journal and your accountability buddy and find a spot where you can sit comfortably and act as a voyeur with a good view to take in the entire scene around you.

When you're ready to start, look around and pick out two or three people you would normally be attracted to and who immediately catch your eye. These people will probably fit into your regular "type." Write down in your journal who you noticed first and what you found attractive about them. These people represent not your true type, but your ego's type. Your ego has created a type that is based on something it is connected to. This can be a type based on your mother or father if you had a good relationship with them. It can be based on your first crush or puppy love if you have a positive association with that person or even an early crush on a celebrity you once idolized.

It is crucial for you to move beyond these types when you are looking to experience true love. These types are based on physical characteristics only, and you must not get stuck in a place of vanity. Your soul is not connected to hair color, physical build, or any other superficial trait, and your soul mate will not necessarily fit into the type that you've been attracted to in the past. Your soul is truly seeking for much deeper and more important qualities in another being.

Now mentally remove from the room this first round of people that you noticed. Pretend that they no longer exist. Go to a second layer and look for two or three people who have a soul and spirit that you find attractive, people who are moving or talking with an energy that appeals to you. You'll notice a dramatic shift in your own energy as you start to look at this second layer of people. This is good—it means that you are no longer looking exclusively with your ego. Write down who you noticed this time and what it was about them that you found attractive. The people you notice this time represent the beginnings of a connection to your spirit and soul's needs. By selecting these people, your inner voice is finally beginning to speak based on the truth of who you are instead of the truth of your previous love script. You may notice right away that you've been paying attention to the wrong things in a mate. That is okay. In fact, it is very good. Trust that you are on the right path as you begin to recognize your soul's true needs instead of your ego's wants.

Now mentally remove from the room the people in your second layer and look around again. This time, you are looking for your soul mate. Tell yourself that your soul mate is really and truly in this room, and that it is up to you to find him or her! As you look around this time, ask yourself, "If the person who is going to love me like I've never been loved before and be the most amazing partner in the world was in this room, who would it be?" It may take you some time to find this person, but be patient. I've never done this with anyone who wasn't able to pick someone out eventually. If you can't find someone, push yourself harder to open your mind to everyone in the room. Let go of your ego's type and your superficial ideas about who you "should" be attracted to. Open not just your mind but your heart and soul, as well. Nine times out of ten, the person my client ends up choosing looks nothing like the people they first noticed. They are often shocked by their own ability to feel so attracted to a completely different type of person.

Once you've found your "test" soul mate, study the person you have chosen and really dissect what it is about him or her that you find attractive. Is it a kindness in the eyes, a warm smile, or the way they are listening, communicating, or acting to the people around them? Write it all down in your journal. The qualities that you'll be writing about now most likely won't have anything to do with looks, although the person you've selected may well be very physically attractive. As I said, this is because your soul is not connected to physicality and the body the way your ego is, and it is voicing its true needs by selecting this person as its mate.

After you are done, go home and sit quietly in a comfortable place and meditate or pray about your love shopping experience. Read through your journal entries about the people you noticed in each round and what you found attractive about each of them.

Reflect on the person whom you ended up choosing as your soul mate and try to keep the qualities you liked about him or her fresh in your mind. When you are done, ask God to bring you the person who you are meant to be with, the person who demonstrates these qualities. Now go out into that world and start putting that newly shifted energy out there. No matter where you go, continue this experiment in your mind. Smile at the people you notice and send them loving energy. Focus on the shift that's happening inside of you and let your mind and ego get used to your new ideas about who your soul mate really is.

So many of my clients undergo a major shift after doing this exercise, so don't be surprised if this happens to you, too. Suddenly, they begin to notice different qualities in the people they meet. Instead of focusing on looks, they are drawn to the qualities they noticed in the person they chose as their soul mate. This is when they start to get really excited about the love God has waiting for them, because they finally understand what they are truly looking for.

It is interesting to note that (generally speaking) this exercise has a much greater impact on women than men. In our society, we often give men a hard time for notoriously wanting certain superficial traits—blond hair, big breasts, or an hourglass figure—but women can be just as critical and superficial, if not more so. They may not voice it in the same way, but this superficiality definitely reveals itself when they go love shopping! Women are so often stuck on that tall, dark, and handsome ideal, and too frequently love the cocky, "bad boy" energy. If a woman's ego is in the way, she may think that she needs that energy in order to feel like she's with a "real man." But when those same women begin listening to their souls, they realize that a man who is truly strong and emotionally intelligent doesn't necessarily come in the physical persona of a *bad boy*.

With men, it's often much easier. They know deep down that they don't really need the big breasts and the perfect features and that what they really need is a woman they can trust and love, who is going to be their rock just as he desires to be hers, and who will ultimately be able to nurture and love them and their children. Physicality is actually much less important to many men than women think. I have done this exercise with countless men who would rather be with a heavier, less beautiful woman who is truly confident and comfortable in her own skin than with a woman who is conceited, rude, or uptight about her looks, yet has a perfect face and body.

One of my most memorable love shopping experiences was with a client of mine named Kelly. She is a beautiful woman, something of a Halle Berry look-alike, and she is at the top of her field. Kelly has a beautiful body and works hard to maintain it, and she insisted that she needed a man with a perfect build, too. Before we went love shopping together, Kelly said to me, "I'm strong and I need a guy who can keep up with me." She thought this meant having a ripped body, a perfect six-pack, and a cocky attitude. This was her type of guy and what she truly believed she needed.

I went with Kelly to a high-end restaurant to do the love

shopping exercise. The place was packed with men, but the first thing Kelly said to me was, "We can't do this tonight. It's not going to work." When I asked her why, she replied, "There aren't any good-looking men here." I looked around and thought that there were a lot of nice-looking men there, but she kept saying, "I don't see anybody." We went around the room and she wrote off every guy I pointed out, saying, "He's out of shape; he looks like he's going through a midlife crisis; that guy has a middle-age tire; he looks dorky with his glasses; that one is balding; he is behind in his style." She was full of superficial judgments for everyone she saw!

I kept pushing Kelly, saying, "You told me that you don't think there are any good-looking guys here, but it's your job to find them. Your guy is actually in this room." She rolled her eyes and looked around again, continuing to dissect each man. Finally she found a few guys who she agreed were handsome. I saw her begin to soften a bit. When I asked her what she noticed about these men, she said things like, "I like his jacket because I can see that he spent a lot of money on it." This told me that she was still looking with her ego. Of course it's okay to value nice things, but they should not be your primary focus when you are trying to find your soul mate!

We moved on to the second layer of men. I told Kelly to find men who had something cute and charming about them, who she might end up liking if she went on a date with them. Her energy softened more, and she picked a few guys out right away. As we went through the layers, Kelly began acting more and more genuine, not only in whom she was selecting but in her own demeanor. Her energy was shifting right in front of me and she became more real and grounded. It was beautiful to watch. She began saying things like, "He's kind of a dork, but his smile is really sweet" or "Even though I never thought I would like a guy who dressed like that, there's something cute about him. I can see that it's his own style." Little by little, Kelly started to connect to her true self and what it wanted and needed in a mate.

When we got to the final layer and I told her to imagine that her soul mate was in the room, she began to seriously scour the restaurant. I saw her eyes go back to one specific guy a few times, and finally she told me that she had found him. The guy she pointed out was kind of chubby, but he had a sweet, "boy next door" face. The thing she really noticed about him, though, was the way he listened to the people he was with. She said, "You can tell that he really cares and that he's a good guy. That's the kind of guy I want to be with." And then she heard herself and exclaimed, "I can't believe I just said that!" She was now staring lovingly at this man whom she had initially dismissed. A few days later, Kelly called me and said, "Now I know that I can be attracted to an entirely different type of guy. This has completely changed me."

This happens with all of my clients to some degree. Very often, I get to this point with my clients and then no longer have to bother finding matches for them, because once they're open to love and attracted to the right people, they are able to find their soul mates on their own. Otherwise, it's very easy when I do match them, because they're able to connect with the right person immediately. As you move forward and begin dating, remember to look for the qualities that you noticed during your love shopping adventure. Read your notes from this exercise often so that your ego doesn't rear its ugly head and try to make its own desires a priority! Most important, continue to pray for God to bring you your soul mate, and He will.

Partner Blueprint

With all the wisdom that you've gained from your love shopping experience, it's time to design your soul mate from your heart rather than your ego. To do this, you're going to create a blueprint for your partner just like the one you created for yourself. I'll include another blank blueprint for you to use for this purpose. This time, write out all the things that you want and need in a partner based on what you learned during your love shopping experience. That's right—you can include wants and needs, as long as you are aware that your true soul mate might not possess all of your wants! You may not be focusing solely on your ego's desires, but you are still of this world. It is okay to include physical attributes that you would prefer in a partner as long as you recognize that the inner person is much more important than any external features.

Before we get started, I want to assure you that focusing on a person's deeper qualities doesn't mean that you have to be with someone you're not attracted to. Some people mistakenly believe that I'm trying to convince them to settle, but it's actually quite the opposite. In fact, when you open yourself up to all people and experiences, you will end up with the person that you really want. You certainly will be physically attracted to that person, but the qualities that you need in order to create a healthy foundation for your relationship must also be there. I'll guide you through creating your partner's blueprint, starting with the outer person and working our way inward.

The Outer Partner

Hair

Your soul mate's hair isn't really going to matter that much, as long as whatever hair they have is healthy, clean, and shows that they know how to honor and care for themselves. However, you can be a little self-focused here and ask for the things you want! Does your soul mate have thick, unruly hair that you can run your fingers through, or neat, fine hair that represents an orderly demeanor? Your soul mate may not have the exact hairstyle that you most prefer, but it's important to include what your ideal partner's hairstyle represents.

Beauty

It may seem strange to talk about beauty when it comes to men (if you are looking for a male partner), but men do possess many different types of beauty. Does your soul mate have a rugged handsomeness or more delicate features? What does your preferred type of male beauty mean to you? Most important, does this person have a sparkle in their eye and an energy that radiates from their smile? Do they show warmth, emotional health, and a connection to the energy of this world through their eyes?

Remember that when you put yourself in this place and then start to look at people who are typically considered "hot," they may suddenly not look so attractive anymore. People who don't love themselves on the inside suddenly won't appear as pretty or handsome to you. Instead, they'll look untrustworthy. Something will be off. You may notice that they photograph well but look much less attractive in person. This represents a shift within you, as you begin to see the world from your soul's perspective rather than your ego's. This is a big step forward, as it is your ego that keeps you stuck.

Health and Wellness

Your ego might have strong opinions about your ideal partner's body, but let your soul take it a bit further than that here and write down what your soul mate's body type represents. Is he or she a health freak who treats their body like a temple, or do they have a healthy balance between good health and fun indulgences? Is he or she active and passionate about sports or more of a homebody? Why is this important to you?

I once met a woman named Kimberly who was gorgeous

both inside and out. Years before, she had met a man named Phil on the phone through business. She had no idea what he looked like, but she felt an immediate connection to him and they fell in love over the phone. They were both curious about what the other looked like, but they were afraid to ask and risk threatening their beautiful connection. When they finally met, Kimberly was disappointed to see that Phil was grossly obese. She immediately thought there was no way she could get involved with him, and she and Phil agreed to remain friends.

As months passed, Kimberly began dating other men who were nice and had more attractive bodies, but she didn't feel nearly the same connection to them as she did to Phil. She kept thinking about him, and finally she called him and asked if he would go on a second date with her. They met in Las Vegas (a middle ground between where each of them lived). On their date, Kimberly realized that she could never be happy with anyone else and that Phil was her soul mate. They ended up eloping that weekend, and have now been happily married for ten years. Kimberly's girlfriends were critical of Phil at first, thinking that she was settling for someone who was beneath her. But after seeing how beautifully he treats Kimberly and hearing from her that they share a wonderful and satisfying sex life, they have broadened their own ideas of who they could be attracted to and all want to find equally wonderful relationships for themselves.

Remember that the package you meet today might not be exactly what you end up with. People grow older, they gain and lose weight, and their styles change. It's much more important to find someone with the deeper soul qualities that will create a healthy and loving relationship. This is what will sustain you.

Clothing, Appearance, and Style

What do your partner's clothes say about them? Do they dress professionally in designer suits, or in more rugged, comfortable clothing? This is obviously about much more than the clothes themselves; it is also about the type of lifestyle that you see your soul mate living. Is he or she a white-collar professional, an artist, or someone who works with their hands? How does this reveal itself in their style? Most important, are they showing the truth of themselves through the way they dress? You are looking for a healthy being, and their wardrobe can provide a clue as to what is going on inside them. What qualities do you want to see radiating through your partner's style?

Face and Skin Care

Does your soul mate have a scratchy beard or is he clean-shaven? What does this say about him on a deeper level? If your soul mate is a woman, does she wear impeccable makeup or have a more natural style? Again, take this deeper and note what your ideas say about this person's spirit as well as appearance. You can tell a great deal about how someone eats and treats themselves by how their skin looks. Are they healthy? Are they taking good care of themselves? If you notice that they take pride in their skin and hair, that's a good sign that they know how to nurture themselves and will be able to similarly care for you.

The Inner Partner

Natural Wisdom

Is your soul mate spontaneous, living from one moment to the next as it comes, or does he or she have everything planned out to the letter? Does he make decisions with his heart or his mind? Does she assess people based on emotions or intellectualism? Why is this important to you? Does he or she have a sense of reality, accountability, and ownership of themselves in this world and society? This is when you will start to notice the red flags that you may have ignored in the past. Use this blueprint to write down the opposite of these warning signs and what you would want to see in a partner instead. This could be someone who is always punctual, who does not gossip about others, or who treats all the people around them with kindness and respect.

Truth

I certainly hope that your soul mate will be truthful not only to you but to everyone in his or her life. Take this a step further and write down how your partner will help you seek the truth in your own life as you learn and grow together. You want to be with someone who tells the truth to other people and, more specifically, who tells the truth to themselves. This is where accountability becomes important. You don't want to end up in a relationship that is perfect until a gripe comes up and then your partner covers his or her ears and refuses to hear the truth. This is far too common. Take this opportunity to express your need for someone who will accept the truth in all aspects of your relationship.

Peace

Is your soul mate calm and easygoing, or does he or she have a more frenetic energy? What brings him or her the most peace in this world? What do these traits say about his true character and spirit? You want to look for someone who has peace in their lives and contentment around them, someone who doesn't have constant drama around them or create drama in their lives. You're looking for a healthy sense of calm and serenity. This doesn't mean that your partner can't have hard days or ever express frustration, but it's very important to note how he or she handles stress. Is this something you wish you had paid more attention to in the past? As you work through your blueprint, take note of the things that you will no longer ignore in the future.

Mind

How does your soul mate engage with the world and stimulate his or her mind? Is he a student of life who is constantly seeking to learn new things and find inspiration, or does he fill his mind with simple pleasures and the intimate knowledge of a few key subjects? Does she have what you would consider a good, sound, balanced mind?

Love

How will your soul mate love you? In what ways will he or she show affection, dote on you? This is incredibly important. How do you deserve to be loved? How will your soul mate prefer to be loved by you? Does this person seem to want the same or similar things as you? How does this person reveal their thoughts about love through the way they speak about their parents and their parents' relationship? This is where your partner's love role models become incredibly important, as what he or she learned is exactly what you will experience.

Ego

What is the state of your partner's ego? Is he or she showy to the outside world or quietly confident, without the need to show off or brag? How will his or her ego manifest itself in your relationship? I speak mostly of ego as if it is negative, but in order to live in this world, we do need to possess an ego. It simply needs to contain a healthy sense of spirit and self. Is this person's ego in check? What is it based on? Does it seem to have a good, balanced energy? Remember that healthy confidence comes from a healthy ego, while conceit and egotism stem from a broken ego.

Your partner's ego should be connected to spirit and wisdom, not selfishness or insecurity.

As you fill out the blueprint for your partner, don't forget to include everything that you need and deserve, no matter what it is. After all the work you've done, this person is going to receive the very best of you, and so you should make sure to get the very best of him or her, too! When you are done, hang your partner's blueprint next to your own completed blueprint as a way of bringing your true self closer to finding your soul mate.

Love Life Blueprint for_____

By the Love Architects

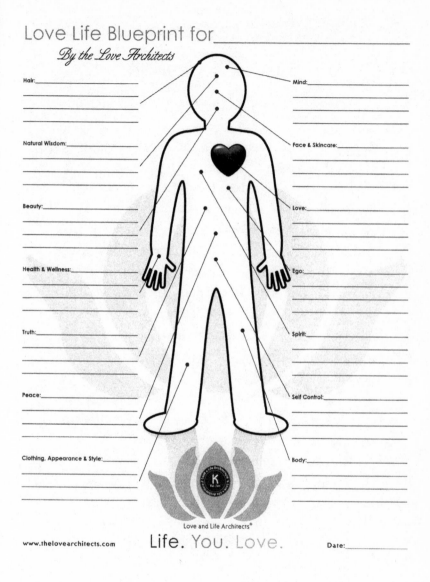

Hair:_____

Natural Wisdom:_____

Beauty:_____

Health & Wellness:_____

Truth:_____

Peace:_____

Clothing, Appearance & Style:_____

Mind:_____

Face & Skincare:_____

Love:_____

Ego:_____

Spirit:_____

Self Control:_____

Body:_____

Love and Life Architects®

www.thelovearchitects.com   Life. You. Love.   Date:_____

HW

HOMEWORK ASSIGNMENT

Partner Vision Board

Once you have had a chance to absorb the experiences of love shopping and filling out your partner's blueprint, I want you to create a vision board for this person. While the qualities that your soul mate should possess are fresh in your mind, this will bring him or her to life for you. Just as with your own vision board, start with a big piece of tagboard and then go through a bunch of magazines that have plenty of pictures of the type of men or women that your new, authentic self is attracted to. Cut out the pictures of people who seem to have the qualities your soul wants in a partner. Instead of just including the sexy guys or girls in the underwear and lingerie ads, this may be the person who's holding a child, laughing with pure joy, or playing with a dog. Tear out as many of these images as you can and glue them on the board.

Next, go through the magazines again, this time looking for images of life experiences that you want to share with your soul mate. This can be a picture of a couple holding a baby, a restaurant you'd like to go to, mountains you want to hike, beaches you want to visit, or anything else that represents life with your soul mate. Tear these images out and put them all up there in a big, beautiful collage. Look at the life you have created on that board. Look at each picture individually and notice the ones that you connect with on a deep level. Take a marker and write down the things that you connect with on each person and each experience. Note exactly what each of them means to you.

When you are done, hang your new vision board up in your bedroom or bathroom—somewhere you will see it every day. Look at it as often as you can, rereading the words that you wrote about each image. Stare at it while you brush your teeth, for a few minutes before going to bed each night, or as the first thing you look at when you wake up in the morning. The more time you spend with these images, the closer you will be to creating this partnership and life for yourself.

CHAPTER NINE
Love Readiness

NOW THAT YOU have completed your love design and understand the qualities that you want and need in a partner, it's time to make sure that you are ready to find him or her and open to receiving the beautiful love that God has waiting for you! Yes, all the work you've been doing throughout this book has helped prepare you to experience true love, but true love readiness takes this transformation to a whole new level. Here are eight steps to becoming truly love-ready and able to welcome the wholeness of love into your life.

Envision Love for Yourself

To be love-ready, you must finally believe in love, and not only believe in it but be able to envision it for yourself. If you are love-ready, you can not only picture love in a wholly positive, sexy, fun, and healthy way, but see it this way in your own life, in a real relationship. In order to be love-ready, you will have rid yourself of the blocks, fears, and sabotages that have kept you from love in the past, whether they were based on your prior relationships, a lack of self-love, or negative images of love that you saw during your childhood or in the media. Now you know what love is and can feel it for yourself.

Let Go of Desperation

Ironically, one huge clue that you are now love-ready is if you no longer feel so desperate to find the kind of loving relationship that you want. You want love, you are excited about it, and you can see it happening, but you don't need it as badly as before, and you don't feel as lonely for it. Your feelings about love are now positive and involve a sense of excitement, hope, and welcoming rather than desperation, fear, and anxiety. In fact, when you are love-ready, you begin to feel more positive about all aspects of your life. You are no longer stuck in the places that you were previously stuck within yourself. You feel joyful, healthy, and at peace with yourself and your life. This is not to say that everything will suddenly be perfect. You may still have stress and frustrations in your life, but you can feel the abundance of love around you no matter how your day is going and whether or not you have a partner.

Radiate Loving Energy

Once you undergo this shift and become love-ready, your new energy will radiate out to the rest of the world. Even the person who is out there waiting for you will feel it, although you haven't met him or her yet! As you approach the world with this loving energy, you will begin to notice the impact you are having on other people. Perhaps your coworkers or members of your family have begun responding differently to you. Remember, this shift doesn't only affect your love life; every aspect of your life will change when you are love-ready. Strangers will begin to smile at you when you pass them on the street, or perhaps a close friend will ask if you've had something done to make you look so refreshed and so much younger! Everyone will notice this new loving energy that you are radiating.

Before long, people will begin to approach you—either to ask you on a date or to introduce you to a single friend of theirs—and, unlike before, you won't feel that initial fear or reluctance that diverts the opportunity. Instead, you'll welcome it and feel excited to go on a date or to meet someone that a friend has in mind for you. If you are someone who would have shunned the idea of a blind date in the past, you'll now welcome any opportunity to meet another soul without any expectations or fears about where it might lead.

Listen to Your Inner Voice

Another sign that you are love-ready is that you can now listen to and truly hear the inner voice that you used to block out because you were afraid of being alone. You can see the warning signs of problematic, unloving behavior in a potential partner sooner and make decisions with wisdom, because you are now in a higher place of self-protection. You have a heightened awareness of who you want around you and will protect yourself from things that lack the healthy, loving energy that you now know you deserve.

Deal with Past Wounds

Issues from your past that have not been dealt with can prevent you from being completely love-ready. However, you can still find love if you aren't fully healed, but you will bring these fears into a relationship with you, so it is important to deal with them before-hand. I'll share the story of my client Stephanie to illustrate how past wounds can keep you from being love-ready. Stephanie came to me very broken and angry. She was adopted as a child and grew up with very loving parents, but she always felt the sting of abandonment. She took it on as her truth that she wasn't lovable, and later stayed married for twenty years before learning that her husband was an alcoholic and a sex addict who had been cheating on her throughout their marriage. After her divorce, she gained a lot of weight and became very bitter and hardened. That is when she came to me.

Stephanie said to me, "I want to believe in love and have the kind of love that my parents had, but I need to understand why I was given up." My work with Stephanie was long and extensive. We hired a detective who found out that her birth mother was only a young teen when she gave birth to Stephanie. Then we did a full life and love design, which helped her gain gratitude for her adoptive parents as well as compassion for her birth mother, who was only a child when she chose to give Stephanie up for adoption. All of this helped her heal tremendously. As she began to feel better about herself, she started to honor herself for the first time in her life, and lost a lot of weight as a result. I noticed her energy shifting and becoming very feminine and lovely. I thought that she might be love-ready.

Finally, I went love shopping with Stephanie, and during the exercise she began projecting a negative, hateful energy that was nothing like the woman I had gotten to know. I realized that she wasn't ready, and we did more work to discover even more pain inside her that hadn't yet been uncovered. Finally, one day she called me and said, "I am so ready to start meeting men," and I could tell that it was really true. Later that night, she called again—this time to say that she had met someone at the grocery store! This is exactly how it works when you are truly love-ready. The love that has eluded you for so long will show up seemingly out of nowhere, and that is because you are finally ready to let love in. In our society, we are told that it is hard to find our soul mates, but it is actually quite easy once you have found yourself.

Shift Your Self-Image

Becoming love-ready doesn't always mean conquering a dramatic, painful past. Sometimes, all it takes is a shift in perception about yourself, love, or even the world around you. Years ago, I had a client named Jack who had been single forever and had never been in a real relationship. He was a classic nerd—a brilliant IT guy who was clueless when it came to style. His hair and facial hair were overgrown to the point that he was hiding behind a long beard and bushy hair, his clothes were out of date, and he was out of shape from leading a sedentary lifestyle.

I could tell that Jack was a total sweetheart inside; he just needed help making his outsides match his insides. We did a full makeover that included new glasses, better-fitting clothes, a cropped haircut, and a sexy goatee. With every stage of the make-over, I could see Jack lighting up more and more. It became clear to me that no one had ever told him that he was good-looking, and as a result he never believed it. As he began to see himself in a new way and other people began to respond to him differently, Jack's natural confidence began to grow. This motivated him to start eating better and exercising, and within only about eight weeks Jack had been completely transformed.

Jack didn't have to overcome a painful childhood or past relationship trauma. In order to be love-ready, he simply needed to believe in his own potential and see that he could be attractive to women. Jack called me and said, "Now I'm ready for you to find someone for me," but by the time I found a girl for him, he had already met someone—and they ended up getting married. You can learn from Jack's story that if you buy into your high school experience or any negative view of yourself, it will become your reality. If you look deeper to find the beauty within yourself and begin to honor it, the rest of the world will honor it, too!

I recently met a woman named Renee who suffered from a similar misconception about herself that was keeping her from experiencing love. Renee was my makeup artist for a publicity appearance. She had big brown eyes and a unique style. The first thing she said to me when we met was, "I have a date tomorrow night that I'm so excited about, but I'm afraid that I'm going to screw it up." My response was, "Well, if you think you will mess it up, then you will." Renee went on to tell me that she was a "dating disaster" who ruined every relationship she had been in. When I pushed to find out where this negative attitude about herself was coming from, she revealed that she had been told by her family and friends that the qualities that made her unique (a quirky sense of humor and self-described "dorkiness") were negative things. Throughout her life, Renee bought into this lie and it became her truth. She looked down on herself instead of letting her natural, silly self flourish.

When I told her that these qualities were adorable and nothing at all to be ashamed of, Renee got very emotional. No one had ever told her that before. After our conversation, Renee was truly excited about her date, and she had a great time and allowed her true self to shine. This is an example of how you can have all of the pieces in place, but still hold yourself back from being love-ready by buying into simple negative messages about yourself. Seeing yourself honestly and lovingly is an extremely important part of being truly love-ready.

Let Go of Excuses That Are Holding You Back

Another step toward becoming love-ready is to put aside the excuses that have been holding you back. These are the reasons you tell yourself that you haven't yet found love. These excuses are fairly universal and common—the divorce rate is so high, my friends are all unhappy in their marriages, my parents had a miserable marriage, all men are jerks, all women just want money, no one would want a single mother with little kids like me, all of the "good ones" are taken. Do these sound familiar? If you have been using any of these excuses, the first thing I need to tell you is that all those fears and excuses are true. The divorce rate *is* high. If your parents' marriage really stunk, then it did. Your friends might truly be unhappy, and so on. This is true, if it's what you want to believe, and it's exactly what you'll get, too. If you believe that your marriage will be unhappy, and then nurture that truth, it certainly will happen. If you believe that the good ones are all taken, then you will sabotage your ability to find the right one and you never will.

But don't forget—the opposite is also true. Half of all marriages do work, and that adds up to a lot of beautiful relationships. Your parents may have ended up being unhappy, but there was a reason they came together in the first place. It wasn't all bad—they had you! Most important, if you believe that there are good men and women out there, then you will be open to finding them, even if you have small children and they never have. We receive what we believe by investing in our belief systems with our attitudes, words, and actions that make them come true.

Learn Your Love Language

Gary Chapman, PhD, has written several books about his theory of the Five Love Languages, or the five main ways in which we each express and feel love. They are: words of affirmation, acts of service, quality time, receiving gifts, and physical touch. Your primary love language is the way that you feel the most loved and protected, and it is essential for you to understand your love language before you can be love-ready. Do you need a partner who will show his or her love by telling you how beautiful and wonderful you are, by doing the dishes, by planning to attend special events together, by buying you tokens of affection, or by holding your hand when you are scared? Do you show your love to others by showering them with gifts, by hugging frequently, by giving them compliments, by cooking big meals, or by spending time together? Remember that your primary love language does not need to be the same as your spouse's, but it is crucial for you and your partner to know what will make the other person feel the most loved.

Love's Building Blocks

I like to look at love and relationships as if they are houses that need to be built on a solid foundation in order to be sound— that's why I named my company The Love Architects. Like an architect building a home, it is my job to make sure that the love in your life is being constructed on solid ground. The building blocks exercise below is a way to check in with yourself and make sure that there are no cracks in the foundation before you begin to build up with love.

Do you remember playing with blocks as a child? Did you experiment with different structures or build straight up to see how high you could go? Either way, I trust that you did it with a sense of wonder and determination, and I want you to hold on to those feelings as you complete this exercise. The building blocks of your relationship represent the values in that relationship and the things that keep you connected to your partner. In order for a relationship to be healthy, each of these values must be present in the foundation. As you go through each term, envision holding a block in your hand that represents it. How does the block feel? Is it heavy or light, rough or smooth? What does it signify to you?

If you feel like making this a truly tactile experience or are in a special place of healing, go out and buy a nice set of wooden blocks and write one of the following words or phrases on each of them. Sit down in a quiet place and pick up one block at a time, taking a few minutes to turn it over in your hands and think about how you can continue to improve in this area. If you are married or in a relationship that needs healing, sit down with your partner and go through the blocks together, discussing each one and what it means to you. Whether you are doing this alone or with a partner, place the blocks (literally or figuratively) in a safe pile when you are done with them, and move forward trusting that they will always be there for you. You will be able to utilize them in your relationship to start building the love that you deserve.

Building Block #1: *Unconditional Love*

This is a pure, sensitive, gentle love, similar to the love that a parent has for a child, and it should be our goal to have unconditional love for our soul mate. Think about how you want to purely love someone and how you want someone to love you unconditionally. What does this mean to you? Remember that you must accept God's unconditional love for you and love yourself unconditionally before you can unconditionally love someone else. If you can't love yourself this way, you will never be able to love someone else to that degree because we can give to others only what we have for ourselves. This doesn't mean that you should start believing you are perfect, but that you love who you are, know your value, and honor it.

Unconditional love is a grown-up and mature love with accountability and self-awareness. It cannot be used to manipulate others by saying, "I would really love him if he made more money," "I love her, but I'm going to hold this over her head," or, "If you really loved me, you would do this or that." Many people question whether or not they should have unconditional love for their partner. What if they do something to hurt you? I believe that if you love someone unconditionally, you will love them even if they do something hurtful. That doesn't mean that you should stay in an abusive or unhealthy relationship! You can take yourself away from a relationship, but if you love someone unconditionally, you don't take your love away. Unconditional love doesn't change and is always there for the other person even if you yourself are not.

Building Block #2: *Gratitude*

I believe that if we are not in a place of gratitude daily, then we are not honoring God. It is so important to put your energy and focus on what is good and has life in it rather than the opposite. Gratitude is essential in every relationship, and the more grateful we are, the more blessings we receive. If you build your foundation without this building block, you will take things for granted. God only gives us what we can handle and what he believes we honor and respect. Every morning, my clients say a prayer of gratitude, and I encourage you to do the same. Name the things that you are grateful for, including being grateful to yourself for putting the work in and doing this for yourself.

If you have had a difficult or painful life, that is no excuse for a lack of gratitude. There are some people who feel sorry for me when they hear that I lived in foster care during my teen years, but I always tell them how grateful I am for the families who cared enough to open their homes and lives to take care of me. What can you find within a painful experience to be grateful for? I find that generally the people who focus on what they have been deprived of lack gratitude most of all, and have a hard time experiencing the fullness of the love around them. What can you take from each moment that God has given you to learn about love and appreciate?

Building Block #3: *Empathy*

Empathy is a way of putting yourself spiritually and compassionately in someone else's shoes to imagine what it is like to feel their pain. It is the opposite of detachment. Empathy is an important building block because it makes up the glue that is needed for bonding. Without that glue, the people in a relationship can become detached from each other and everything will fall apart when the going gets rough.

Empathy has been an important building block in my own relationship. Lance and I both came into our marriage with our own childhood wounds, and it is the understanding that we each have of each other's wounds that has kept us connected. Lance was made the "man of the house" at age five to meet his mother's emotional needs. It was too much pressure for him to grow up thinking it was his job to take care of others' needs rather than his own. While loving women, he found himself resenting them because he felt that he needed to always act the caretaker. Early in our marriage, I tried to "take care of him" in different ways, when he was sick, sad, stressed, and it became uncomfortable for him because he wasn't used to being vulnerable. We fought about this often in the beginning because I took it personally. As I realized that this was simply a part of his love script, I found empathy for his pain. It's not my job to parent him or to replace the love and nurturing that he missed out on as a child, but I can love him as an adult and have compassion so that he has room to do his own healing.

Building Block #4: *Acceptance*

In order to build a foundation with someone, you must accept them for who they are without trying to change them. If you love someone but need them to change a few things in order to be with you, then they're not the right one for you. Of course, you must accept yourself before you can expect anyone else to accept you. If there are things that you cannot accept about yourself, then you're not love-ready yet. Although there are some things that you can't (and shouldn't) accept in another person. Nobody is perfect, so you will have to dissect the things that bother you to determine if they are deal-breakers that go against your value system and can hurt you, or just things that bug you. The things that bother you in a relationship may simply represent something that is broken inside you. As you work on healing that wound within you, you'll release that judgment toward your partner.

Building Block #5: *Charity*

Because of the balance on earth that may not always seem so fair, there is always someone who has more than you and someone who has less. All of us have a spiritual obligation to acknowledge those who are in need. There are so many ways to give back. We can do so with kindness (a smile or prayer), with our time (volunteering), or with money (simply writing a check). While all of these are important, I believe that it is essential to give our energy and time to those in need. At the end of the day, we're all one, and charity is an important building block because it brings us all closer together and improves your ability to experience full love. It's when we're in a place of giving the most of ourselves that we can give the most of ourselves in love, and this is when we can also receive it!

Building Block #6: *Friendship*

You need to have a strong friendship with yourself first so that you can develop healthy friendships with others and ultimately with your partner. It all begins with you. Do you treat yourself as a best friend or do you cut yourself down and act more like an enemy? Once you can be your own best friend, you can build true friendships with other people that are absent of judgment and competition. This same healthy friendship is what you are striving for in a relationship, but you cannot build it into your foundation until you have it with yourself.

Building Block #7: *Kindness*

It is so important to remember to be kind to one another, as well as to ourselves. Many people are kind to themselves in ego, but this is a disconnected sense of kindness. Being in love with ourselves based on a superficial nature can create a disconnection from the true awareness that can lead to kindness. True kindness involves all the other building blocks, and is therefore essential in bringing together a healthy foundation for love.

HW

HOMEWORK ASSIGNMENT

Go on a Test Date

Take some time to think about whether or not you feel that you are love-ready and to complete the building blocks exercise. When you are ready, you can continue to assess your progress by going on a test date!

First, you must find your love mission "date" either by looking online, asking a friend to set you up, or meeting someone in your daily life. This could also be a great time to invest in a "respected" dating service. Try not to put too much pressure on yourself or your date. Remember that it is only a test, but at the same time, you never know when and where you will find your soul mate. If you really are love-ready, this could very well end up being the one! Make sure that while you're on the date, you are being authentic and staying true to the *real* you. Seek to understand the person you are with, even if you know that it won't go any further than the one date. Pay attention to how you feel the entire time, and then go home and write in your journal about the experience. Did you feel accepted and were you accepting of them? Did you notice a shift in your energy, compared to how you felt on previous dates? What did you notice about the other person that you may not have picked up on in the past?

No matter how the date itself goes, trust that you are on the path to finding love and that you become more and more love-ready every day. Congratulations for doing the work and sticking with it!

CHAPTER TEN

Real Love, Right Now!

B ASED ON ALL the work and healing that you have done so far, I'm sure you can feel the full experience of love coming closer to you each and every step of the way. Take a moment to think about where you are now compared to the places that you were stuck before you began reading this book. Unless you need to go back and do some more healing, you are now love-ready and should feel a huge shift happening within you. It is very possible that after doing all of this work, you have already found the type of relationship you were looking for! As I mentioned, at this stage of the process, many of my clients are so wide open and receptive that they end up finding their soul mates on their own.

If this hasn't happened to you yet, know that love already

surrounds you and trust that your soul mate is right around the corner. I'm serious! Start each morning with a prayer that today you will connect with God to bring all the love around you into your life! No matter where you go. Know that your sexy, amazing, loving, fun, warm, exciting guy or gal is out there waiting for you, and be excited about meeting him or her! With this energy, you will be wide open, and at this point finding love will be all about radiating that energy in every moment of your life. As I've said before, you have no idea where or when you will end up finding your soul mate! It could happen at the car wash, at church, while out for a run, at the dry cleaner's, at the coffee shop while standing in line, or at a singles event. Every time you walk out the door, remember that love might find you at any moment. If you show up for every part of your life radiating loving, peaceful energy, the right person will find you. But that doesn't mean that the work is over and you can just sit back and wait for the love of your life to come to you! Just as you must be proactive in order to find a job or stay in shape, you must go after what you want when it comes to love, beginning with faith!

There are millions of people in this world, and so often we pass each other like ships in the night. We all want to experience love, but we're afraid to connect and we sometimes forget to take note of those around us. It would be so easy to just walk past your soul mate on the street without even noticing him or her. Being proactive when it comes to love means remaining aware of others and open to a connection at any time. Even if you are actively looking for love, it often comes when you least expect it. You may have just rolled your eyes at the idea that you could find your soul mate at the dry cleaner's, but it very well could happen that way! You have to make yourself available in all areas. That means remaining spiritually and emotionally available at all times and places, but it also means putting yourself in multiple situations where you might find someone. It's not enough to just sit back and wait for love to come to you; you must also put yourself out there! I know many Christians who hesitate to do so because they are waiting for God to bring the right person to them. This reminds me of one of my favorite parables, which actually has a really deep meaning, so I'm happy to share this parable with you now:

It was flooding, and as the floodwaters were rising, a man was on the stoop of his house when another man in a rowboat came by. The man in the rowboat told the man on the stoop to get in and he'd save him. The man on the stoop said, no, he had faith in God and would wait for God to save him. The floodwaters kept rising and the man had to go to the second floor of his house. A man in a motorboat came by and told the man in the house to get in because he had come to rescue him. The man in the house said no thank you. He had perfect faith in God and would wait for God to save him. The floodwaters kept rising. Pretty soon they were up to the man's roof and he got out on the roof. A helicopter then came by and lowered a rope; the pilot shouted down to the man on the house to climb up the rope because the helicopter had come to rescue him. The man on the house wouldn't climb the rope. He told the pilot that he had faith in God and would wait for God to rescue him. The floodwaters kept rising and the man on the house drowned. When he got to heaven, he asked God where he went wrong. He told God that he had perfect faith in God, but God had let him drown. "What more do you want from Me?" asked God. "I sent you two boats and a helicopter."

When clients say to me, "It was hard for me to decide to come to you because it feels like I'm going against God's plan," I always ask them, "How do you know I'm not part of God's plan? The truth is that God has given you (and continues to give you) everything that you need in order to experience love, joy, and to have prosperity. He gave you the tools you need, and he wants you to use them, so don't be afraid to be proactive when it comes to getting what you want in life!"

Although I have never been a huge fan of online dating because of some of the unsavory people (or, I should say, unhealed, disconnected people who either don't know themselves or lack downright honesty) on those sites, there are some good people to be met online. People really can find their soul mates online, so go ahead and look there, as I can now say that after all the hard work you've done thus far, you'll make healthier choices! However, it's also important to go out into the world with this new energy of yours—don't just hide it behind your computer at home. Accept invitations that come your way. Go to parties, singles events, and all sorts of social gatherings. Continue to ask your friends to introduce you to their contacts and expand your own social circle.

Attend these events with the same authenticity and energy that you will now radiate at work, on the phone, and while you're driving down the street. Wherever you are, be present and aware at every moment. Don't hide your feelings or your true self—

smile at others if you happen to meet their eyes, say hello, or strike up a conversation whenever the opportunity arises. This energy will make you approachable no matter where you are or what you're doing, so don't be surprised if people begin to come up to you and start a conversation. While many people claim that reading a book or listening to an iPod on the train or in a coffee shop may make you seem unapproachable, if you have the right energy, there is nothing that can truly make you unapproachable. Even being completely engrossed in your book won't stop a man who notices you from coming up and saying, "You look like you're really into that book—tell me about it." While in the past, your earbuds may have made people think, "He really looks like he doesn't want to be disturbed," your energy is different now, and your results will be different!

Love Scouting

Of course, it's not enough to send out good energy and only expect others to approach you. In order to be truly open to finding love, you must approach others with the same genuine, confident energy that you now possess. With my clients, I act as their love scout at this stage in the process, using all the information that we learned during the love shopping experience and often while creating their partner blueprint. Now I am going to walk you through how to be your own love scout so that you never need to hire a matchmaker!

Just as with the love shopping and blueprint exercises, you

aren't going to do this alone. It will be helpful if you can find one or two additional love scouts. These should be people whom you respect, who have love in their own lives, and who seem to understand you. Gather these people and tell them that you are in the process of bringing an amazing relationship into your life and that you would appreciate their support and partnership. You'll likely be surprised by how much everyone (including men) enjoys playing matchmaker, especially for someone they love.

Love scouting is all about looking for the qualities that you picked up on during your love shopping experience, so make sure to tell your love scouts about the deeper qualities that you ended up finding so attractive. Better yet, why not turn this into a really fun girls' or guys' night out? Gather your love scouts and take them to a busy restaurant or club—somewhere similar to where you originally went love shopping—and love shop together! Lead them through the exercise and have them do it for themselves, too, even if they are married or in relationships. It will be beneficial for them to experience this firsthand and give them a deeper understanding of the qualities that you are really looking for in someone. After your night out, tell them to start love scouting for you based on that experience. They'll likely be excited to scout for you in their own offices, churches, and daily lives.

In the meantime, you are also going to act as your own scout. When you are out and about, use your love shopping skills to narrow down who you want to approach. If you see a man across the room who you think is attractive, sit back for a minute and do your assessment based on what you learned when you originally went love shopping. Read his body language and energy. Pay attention to how he responds to the people around him. Does he seem authentic, passionate, sweet, and fun? Does he possess the qualities that you noticed during the first and second rounds of love shopping, or when you had to narrow it down to find "the one"? Of course, this doesn't mean that you have to disregard the person's physical qualities. You are looking for someone who is attractive to you on all levels.

If you find someone who fits the bill and isn't wearing a wedding ring or other sign of commitment, simply approach them! You don't need a cheesy or rehearsed pickup line. Instead, say something honest and genuine like, "I noticed something cool about your eyes," or, "You have such a sweet smile," or, "You give off a really intriguing energy." When you call out things like this on a real, spiritual level, people will respond sincerely. They will take it as a compliment and thank you. Most often, they will engage you in conversation and connect with something similar in you. During these interactions, always remember to be 100 percent *you*—the real, authentic you.

The person you approach may end up being married or in a relationship, but they will undoubtedly still be thankful that you took the time to compliment them on something genuine. Don't ever look at this as a failure or wasted energy. You never know—this person's best friend could end up being your soul mate. When you do this, you must be open to any possibility. If the person ends up being rude, unwelcoming, or otherwise different from what you expected, just leave them with the compliment, thank them for their time, and walk away. Unfortunately, not everyone wears their wedding ring, so the person you approach might end up being married. Regardless, always leave the situation looking back on it as a positive learning experience.

When I go out love scouting for one of my clients, I do it with focused intention. Based on their desired qualities that revealed themselves when we went love shopping, I go to a location that is likely to have good matches for my client. When I find someone who looks like a fit, I approach them and say that I am a Love Architect who is in the business of creating healthy relationships and that I have someone whom I'd like to possibly introduce them to. It's up to you whether or not you want to go on love scouting "expeditions" like this or just do the scouting wherever you normally find yourself in life. Either way, love scouting for yourself should never feel burdensome or like a job. Don't approach the expeditions with desperation or anxiety. They should be fun and exciting! Also remember that if you go out on these expeditions and come up dry, it's fine. The good news is that your person is right around the corner. The relationship that you want is closer than ever before, so don't pressure yourself or feel like you are working under any kind of deadline.

Trust your intuition about people when you are out love scouting. It's amazing how much you can pick up on by simply focusing on someone's energy. I once went scouting for a male client who wanted a woman with a sassy, confident spark, but who was also a devout Christian. At a local coffee shop, I noticed a strikingly beautiful woman who was tall, blond, and looked like a model. But it wasn't her looks that made me think that she would be a fit for this client. She had an easy spirit about her and a sparkle in her eye that I knew he would like.

I approached the young woman and said, "You're such a lovely woman with a unique presence about you. Tell me, are you in a relationship?" At first, she thought that I was interested in her, and boldly asked me, "Is this for you?" I knew for sure that my client would like this confident attitude. We kept talking, and it turned out that she had just graduated from a Christian college. I introduced her to my client and they ended up getting married. There was no way for me to tell by looking at her that she had all the qualities that my client was looking for, but her energy seemed to match his, and I was right.

If you like the idea of going on intentional love scouting expeditions, simply go somewhere you think your type of person is likely to be, pick out the people with the most attractive energy, and approach them. If this isn't something that appeals to you, that is absolutely fine. You can still be your own love scout by heightening your awareness and being open in the places you go to on a regular basis. Show up at these places authentically, and put your best self forward by making sure that you are always clean and well groomed. No, this doesn't mean that you need full makeup every time you leave the house, but it does mean that you should take pride in your appearance wherever you go, even if it's just for a minute. I know so many women who wonder why they can't find a man, but who regularly go out wearing frumpy clothes. Your outside appearance reflects how you feel on the inside, so make sure that you are always honoring yourself in the way you groom yourself and dress.

Never force this by making yourself go to places you wouldn't normally find yourself or that don't fit with your values or life-style. At the same time, keep in mind that the spiritual and emotional place in which you are looking for love is much more important than the physical place. You can literally meet your soul mate anywhere, but not if you're searching from a place of ego or brokenness. Don't look backward and become tempted to go back to an old relationship. Think about how much you've changed since that relationship ended. It will no longer serve the new, authentic you.

Keep in mind that fears may crop up even after you have become love-ready. The important thing is to acknowledge and honor where these fears are coming from and let them come out if they need to. Don't let them hold you back. I recently spoke to a client who had met a man online that she was very excited about. The more she told me about him, the more hopeful I be-came for her. He seemed to be a great match for her and he was obviously crazy about her, too. But as I started to become ex-cited, she began belittling the whole thing and saying, "Oh, it probably won't work out." When I asked her what she meant, she said, "He seems like the kind of guy who's dated really beautiful women." I said, "What are you talking about? What happened to all the work we did?" She started to become really emotional. Finally, she admitted, "I'm just so scared." Sometimes, it's really scary to receive what we've always wanted. This happens all the time—couples who tried so hard to get pregnant suddenly panic when they finally succeed. We all have fears, and if you are afraid of getting what you want, then acknowledge your fear, and move on. I told this client to go on the date and simply enjoy herself!

Don't make more of these things than they really are. Move forward from anything that is negative or painful and focus on what is positive, wonderful, lovely, and true. Remember that you're in a good place right now! Just continue to live your life and have fun without focusing too much on your search for love. More than anything, enjoy the new relationship you now have with yourself and listen to your inner voice, as this will guide you better than any advice I could ever give! If you wake up one day feeling like you don't want to think about finding love today, honor that. If you trust in God and trust in yourself, you are going to find your partner when and where you should, not when you decide to force it. If you feel like staying in one day or dressing like a slob to go out one night, go ahead. The funny thing is, you might end up meeting your soul mate that same day, regardless. How you love yourself is most important. As you work as your own love scout, focus more on finding yourself than on finding another person. If you know who you are and authentically love yourself, the full experience of love will come your way!

HW

HOMEWORK ASSIGNMENT

Court Yourself

It's possible that you've done all the work in the book so far, and yet you feel in some ways like you are still stuck and nothing is working for you. It's okay. I have faith in you! Even if perhaps you don't feel the transformation happening yet within you, don't give up! It does not mean that you are destined to be alone. Just take some time to think about what is going on inside you. It is possible that your love readiness work has triggered something *else* in you that needs to be healed before you can move on! This happens sometimes and is completely normal.

A client of mine, Kelly, had a huge breakthrough during my love shopping exercise but went on to begin new unhealthy patterns soon afterward and started sabotaging all of her relationships. She simply wasn't ready yet. She had gained great knowledge and needed to spend more time healing herself before she would be ready for a relationship. If this happens to you, I suggest that you begin courting yourself as a step toward healing. This is also a wonderful thing to do for yourself even if you feel that you have shifted. Loving and caring for yourself in this way can only help call love closer to you.

To begin, take yourself out on a date. It may sound

silly. Think about it this way—if *you* don't think it's fun to be with you, how can you expect someone else to enjoy it? Make a reservation at a restaurant you've been dying to go to. Look through your closet and pick out something that you'd love to wear on a date, and then do your hair and makeup as you would for a special occasion. Go out and spoil yourself rotten for one night. Eat and drink whatever you'd like, and enjoy your own company while taking note of the people around you. You never know—you might end up meeting your soul mate while you're on a date with yourself! Members of the opposite sex are often drawn to those who have the confidence to spend time alone.

Follow up your dinner date by taking yourself to a really fun movie. Fully enjoy yourself and then go home and cuddle up in your bed with your journal. Write about your night, what you enjoyed, which parts may have felt uncomfortable, what you may have observed in other couples around you, and what you've learned from the entire experience. Repeat this on a regular basis as an important way of nurturing yourself and preparing you to receive someone else's love.

FIVE-DAY LOVE REALITY CHECK

Chances are, you are now completely love-ready. You feel different, and you also are really beginning to see yourself and others differently! You feel more confident and are starting each day with more enthusiasm. I have no doubt that others have also been noticing this shift within you. Have friends and colleagues mentioned how great you look or that you seem rested and content? As you become a more joyful, loving person and embrace your own beauty, you are noticing the beauty in others more! You have a much keener sense of what you are looking for in a partner, and members of the opposite sex are starting to notice the fresh, new, loving energy radiating from you. I'm sure you've caught people checking you out at the grocery store, at work, or even from the car sitting next to yours in traffic. Enjoy these moments as you continue to prepare yourself to find the one! That is, if you haven't already found him or her! Regardless, keep reading; there's important work to do still. Remember, it's not just about finding your true soul mate; it's also about experiencing and *keeping* the amazing bond and relationship you will share.

DAYS 21–25

CHAPTER ELEVEN

Dating Authentically

AT THIS POINT, I trust that you are relishing your new relationship with yourself and enjoying meeting potential partners while you are out living your life. That is wonderful and I commend you for sticking with it and accomplishing so much on our journey together thus far. As you continue to meet people and date them, you will be acting as your own love scout all the while. It's likely that you are meeting people all the time in a way that now feels completely natural. This is of course due to the fact that you are now showing up as your authentic self instead of leading with your ego. It is your acceptance of God's love and your newfound love for yourself that attract others to you and will eventually draw your soul mate into your life.

Tradition and Courting

When it comes to dating, I am what some people consider to be "old-fashioned," and I believe strongly in the tradition of courting. "Courting" is the dating process, the important experience you share while finding out if this person is someone you want to be in a relationship with or let alone even spend your life with. This is the time when you should be focusing on getting to know each other, good and bad, warts and all! In my experience of finding love for thousands of men and women, I have learned that the vast majority of both men and women still want to maintain the old-fashioned dating traditions. Women long to be courted and men yearn to do it, but too many of them don't know what this even means anymore. I believe that courting is simply a gentle, genuine, and necessary way for a man and a woman to get to know each other and discover if they desire to experience love with each other.

Today's society sadly lacks so much tradition, especially when it comes to dating and relationships. It has become common and acceptable for women to ask men out and pay for dates, for communications throughout the dating process to take place through text messages or e-mail, and for men and women to sleep together on the first (or second or third) date. I believe in many ways it is this lack of tradition that has gotten us into so much trouble and led in part to today's staggering divorce rates. Many of us forget that there is a reason for tradition. It provides a structure that both men and women need in order to keep their relationships healthy and balanced.

Chivalry is one important tradition and a part of courting that is severely lacking in our society. I have heard this complaint from thousands of men over the past twenty years, and my dear friend and *New York Times* bestselling author of *The Manual: A True Bad Boy Explains How Men Think, Date, and Mate—and What Women Can Do to Come Out on Top,* "Relationship Mechanic" Steve Santagati couldn't have said it better. "Without an opportunity to act chivalrous, men are now losing the chance to act and feel like men while courting women. Men are becoming more like women and women more like men." When a women does not allow a man to act chivalrous by holding the door for her or pulling out her chair, many times the man feels that he has lost his place and his purpose in the process of courting. Men truly want to do these things and become confused when they are told not to. After working with thousands of men and talking to them about this very topic, I am convinced that we must return to chivalry and traditional roles when it comes to courting and relationships.

Some women do not feel comfortable with the idea of being courted. Perhaps you are groaning out loud or rolling your eyes as you read this, thinking, "I don't need a man to do these things for me." If this is the case, it might help to take a moment to check in with yourself and find out why simple acts of chivalry make you feel so uncomfortable. Do you feel you would be giving up something by allowing a man to court you? Why do you feel this way? The truth is that you give nothing away by letting a man treat you kindly, and if you are truly confident and secure, you won't feel threatened by this. In all actuality, you would enjoy it. Remember that there are reasons that things have worked a certain way for so many years, and reasons that we as a society are more broken now than ever.

While I personally believe in traditional male and female roles in a relationship, this does not mean that I place one partner in a position of power over the other. On the contrary, all healthy relationships should be built on a foundation of mutual respect and admiration. My husband is the head of our household, but he does not hold power over me, nor does he want to. However, I do give him the power of influence, which he deserves. I am a strong woman and we treat each other mutually with the respect that we each deserve. It can be especially lovely for a strong woman who has learned how to be self-sufficient to have a man who can also treat her like a lady and be her rock. A strong man can be her safe place where she can let her soft, feminine side show. Many women today have grown so accustomed to a lack of chivalry that they don't know how to respond when a man tries to act chivalrous. I have been guilty of this myself! My husband is very chivalrous, which I love, but I am so used to traveling alone and doing most everything for myself that when we are out together he has to literally run to beat me to the door so that he can open it for me. This recently happened at a restaurant and he asked me, "Can you please just let me be a gentleman with you?" This reminded me yet again of how important it is for men to have a place and a way of showing their respect by acting chivalrous toward women.

While I encourage everyone to approach other people as a

part of being their own love scout and just being a friendly and open human being, I do not think it's best for a woman to ask a man on a date. When a woman is the one pursuing the man, it creates an imbalance and the man often loses interest fast. The same thing goes for paying. I believe the man should pay for the date and (in general) offer to pay for everything while he is courting a woman. Before you throw this book across the room and accuse me of being sexist and out of touch, let me give you an example that illustrates why this is so important.

I once had a client named Lucy who asked a man named Seth out on their first date. She did all the planning and even paid for the date. This completely confused Seth. He was attracted to Lucy, but he thought that because she asked him out and paid, she was only interested in him as a friend. Meanwhile, Lucy felt a connection to Seth, too, and she didn't understand why he never asked her out again after this first date. This pattern continued for quite a while, with Lucy calling and asking Seth out and taking on a male role in their relationship. After receiving feedback from both sides, it was clear that they both wanted to be together but they weren't being honest about their real feelings, and both became very confused as a result! When they *finally* told each other how they felt, they tried to start over by going on a "real" date, with Seth taking on the traditional male role, but by this time it felt completely awkward. They didn't know how to shift into traditional roles, even though this is what both of them had wanted all along.

I advocate for traditional roles while you are dating, but I don't want it ever to feel disingenuous, as if you are actually playing a role. Remember that the whole point is for you to be your most authentic self the whole time you are courting. This needn't be contradictory—there is room here to compromise by following my basic guidelines while always doing what feels natural to you. Therefore, if a man asks you out and pays for the first date, you can offer to treat the next time if you want. This is a sign of respect and a very nice gesture, but if he insists on paying, I recommend that you let him. But don't get upset if he takes you up on your offer! That's playing games and not being genuine. Most men won't accept, however; most feel that a woman's gesture of offering to pay is good enough. They appreciate it but really do feel more comfortable if they are allowed to fulfill their traditional role by paying for each date. It is what most men are taught to do from a young age and the easiest way they know to show respect. You are not being bought and you do not owe a man anything if he takes you out on a date. It is letting him show you that he honors you, and letting him take that role shows that you recognize you are worthy of his respect.

In case you think that this feels out of touch and is only appropriate for the older generations, I want to share my twenty-five-year-old son's most recent dating experience. He was at work waiting tables when he met a very attractive young woman named Laura. Laura was flirtatious from the very beginning and my son was attracted to her. His plan was to gather the courage to approach her and ask her out, but before he had a chance, Laura approached him and very boldly and confidently asked him to go out with her later that same night. My son was flattered and intrigued, but he felt taken aback by the role reversal. He decided to give her a chance, and said yes. Laura responded by immediately insisting, "Give me your number." When my son told me this story, I knew right away that Laura was into power plays. That is why she acted so aggressively with a man she just met for the first time.

My son tried to turn things around and asked Laura for her phone number, instead. She relented, and the two of them made plans to meet up at a brewery later that night. After they parted ways, he felt a bit uncomfortable about the whole interaction. Even worse, because she clearly liked him, he felt guilty, as if he should have enjoyed being pursued like this, but didn't. He decided to send Laura a text, suggesting that they meet up on another night instead, as things had been planned without much thought. This was his way of trying to regain some control over the situation. When I asked him why he texted her instead of calling, he admitted that although he was attracted to her, he had already lost a little bit of respect for her. He told me that when he or one of his friends sends a text instead of calling a girl early on, it is generally either because they aren't taking her seriously, not overly interested, or they're afraid of rejection.

This is precisely why texting is never a good way to communicate in the beginning of a relationship or is a good sign that things are already off in a bad direction when it comes to healthy communication. It's merely a convenient method of avoidance. Laura texted back saying that she would "love to" but would be "busy" for the rest of the month. Clearly, she was playing games. Now she was trying to make my son feel like a hunter who had to chase her even though she was *still* in a position of power. It worked, and he began to feel intrigued. They went ahead with their date as originally scheduled by her.

My son told me that once Laura arrived for their date, everything about her seemed too good to be true. She looked beautiful and sexy in an appropriate way, dressed in a classy wrap dress with cute tall boots. Her hair was shiny and natural, and she wasn't wearing too much makeup or perfume. As they talked, he learned that they had a lot in common and that she was very smart and well spoken. Everything about her was perfect, but he couldn't get their initial meeting out of his head. He also realized that even though he was transfixed by Laura, he never got a word in during their date! She didn't ask him anything about himself the whole night. Does this sound familiar to you? Is this the behavior of someone you know? Pay close attention as you read on.

When my son eventually ended the date, Laura immediately said, "I would love to see you again. Would you like that?" This made him feel uncomfortable yet again, but he said yes and ended up seeing her again the very next night. Once again, Laura picked the restaurant and took control of everything. He felt more and more uncomfortable, and found himself wondering what their relationship would be like if they ended up together. Would she be in control of every decision? Sure enough, on that second date, Laura began to talk about their future together, and my son knew then that it wouldn't go any further. At the end of the date, Laura asked, "Aren't you going to kiss me?" When he leaned in for a little kiss, she wrapped her arms around him and kissed him passionately. He was so turned off by how aggressive and sexual this was that he awkwardly broke off the kiss and said good night.

My son asked me later, "She has so much going for her. Why is she so desperate?" Sure enough, her aggression seemed like desperation and really served to turn him off. After their second date, Laura began calling him frequently, acting vulnerable and completely different from the girl he had met. When he didn't respond, Laura finally said that this happened to her all the time and it proved that all guys are jerks. I chose to share this story with you because so many women act like this and then come up with excuses for their behavior like "All men are jerks" or "He's just intimidated by my great career." The truth is that there are tons of wonderful men out there who are not intimidated by strong women or good careers, but they are repelled by the aggressive energy that women like Laura are sending off.

To answer my son's question, she might have acted like this as a result of growing up believing that her power comes from her prowess or looks. If she is accustomed to being noticed, she might feel a need to get that same attention from a man. But the bottom line is that it doesn't work. Attracting soul to soul is about purity and balance, not games or power plays. Perhaps you are reading this and thinking, "But it is just my personality to act more aggressive. It would be inauthentic to act differently." If this is the case, then you are still disconnected from your authentic self. I have dealt with some of the people with the largest egos in the world, and they are the ones who end up becoming the biggest softies when they finally connect to themselves. If any of this rings true to you, push harder to find out why you feel the need to hold so much power in your relationships. You must find the answer before you can experience true love.

After each date, both women and men should feel comfortable calling the other person to say thank you. This isn't a manipulative or intentional step but simply a question of kindness and manners. I don't believe in playing games of any kind, so there is no need to wait a certain number of days before calling someone. Whenever you feel like it, pick up the phone and say thank you for the date. If you had a good time, say so. Women who feel compelled to can even go as far as saying, "I'd love to see you again," but you should wait for the man to officially ask you on the next date.

Women, don't worry that if you don't ask a man out on the next date he won't know that you're interested and refrain from asking you out again. A man who is confident and secure will ask you out because he simply wants to see you again. He won't waste time reading into what you do or don't say. If he is analyzing your behavior and doubting himself, that is his own brokenness revealing itself. Trust in the experience that you had on the date and trust in God's plan for you. Don't spend time waiting and wondering why you haven't heard from someone. If a man fails to ask you out again, let it go. All the doubt and speculating that goes on between dates is just chatter in your mind that serves only to confuse you further. Trust, have patience, and let the rest unfold.

Sex and Dating

While you are dating and trying to discover whether or not a person is the right one for you, nothing can confuse matters more than sex and intimacy. That is why I feel very strongly that you will have the best chance for success in your marriage if you wait to have sex until you are married. No matter how sexually active you may (or may not) have been in the past, holding off from becoming intimate in a new relationship will give you a real opportunity to clearly evaluate whether or not this person is right for you in a way that you've never done before. Will everyone who reads this book follow this advice? Of course not. But my goal is to give you the best chance at success in your marriage, and I believe that you will have that chance only if you choose to wait.

It's so easy to meet someone and feel incredible chemistry very early on. These feelings may make you think that this person really is "the one," and that you want to get intimate as a new way of connecting. While this is natural, it is simply your body's chemicals playing tricks on you. It's impossible to really know if this person is right for you in the beginning, when you haven't had any real experiences together yet. You haven't faced any challenges together—of course it has all been fun and easy! Your pheromones are going wild and you very well might end up having incredible sex with this person, but this would only make you feel more confused. If you connect intimately, you might become convinced that he or she is your soul mate even if you were never meant to be together. It is easy to have sex—it is even easy to have great sex—but it is much more difficult to build a lasting marriage, and that is what I am trying to help you do.

Even if you know in your heart that you have met your soul mate, you must be wise and proceed differently than you have in the past in order to give this relationship a fair chance. Intimacy makes everything else seem more meaningful than it is. Someone you might have ended up losing interest in after two or three dates could turn into your spouse or the parent of your child if you get intimate too soon. It will cause you to attach too much meaning to the relationship. Of course sex is important within a marriage, but it is not the foundation for a relationship or a marriage. There is a reason I did not list it as one of the building blocks. There is so much you need to learn about a person before letting sex cloud your judgment and you must build your relationship on a solid foundation before becoming intimate.

One of my sisters recently married a man who is now a devout Christian. Although before meeting each other they were both sexually active, when they got together they decided that they would wait until marriage to have sex. These two beautiful, sexual beings were able to wait and build their relationship on a foundation of friendship. They are very happily married today and this is a testament to the power of waiting.

I know that some of you might read this and wonder if I am being hypocritical, as I obviously didn't wait until marriage in some of my own relationships. The truth is that by getting intimate too soon, I never gave those relationships a chance to truly reveal themselves or to grow without becoming focused on, although using protection, an unplanned pregnancy. Although I wouldn't change having had my sons for the world, my lack of ability and self-awareness hurt them in many ways in the process. I have two sons who will never know what it's like to have their mom and dad together, who weren't given the opportunity for a full sibling, and missed out on the stability they each deserved, having a mother who was still trying to figure out love and life.

I realize that many people will not be able to follow my advice perfectly, but I want to focus on giving you the best experience possible, and that is what you will have if you wait. In our society today, there is much more brokenness and confusion that stem from people rushing into bed too soon. In order to give yourself your best chance at real love, right now, you should protect your spirit, soul, and body by waiting for sex until marriage. If the person you are with doesn't agree, then they are not the right person for you! They should care more about your values and what is important to you than simply getting in your pants!

Sequence of Dates

Now that you have a general sense of my dating guidelines and the role that I believe you should play during the courting process, I am going to break down your first few dates and give my advice for how to have the best experience on each date while always staying true to yourself.

Pre-Date

This is the first time you two will meet again after your initial meeting. If you were introduced to this person through a friend or a website, this may be the first time that you meet in person at all. I recommend that you meet for this pre-date during daylight hours somewhere you can really talk, such as a casual restaurant at lunchtime or a coffee shop. It should be light and informal. You are really just using this opportunity to find out if you feel connected to this person at all. Avoid talking about deep, heavy things unless they come up in a natural manner and don't turn it into an intense interview. Instead, just check this person out—get a sense of their attitude and energy. Take note of how he or she treats others. On this date, I don't recommend that either of you consume any alcohol because you can't be your genuine selves if you are under the influence. Simply show up authentically and see if you two have a connection.

Don't put too much pressure on this meeting and don't attach much meaning to it. Just be yourself, have fun, and see how it goes! I do recommend that you set a cutoff time for this date—anywhere from half an hour to two hours. If, after two hours, you still feel any connection to this person and want to spend more time together, you should move on to a "real" first date. I do not recommend much physical contact during the pre-date. Remember, you do not want to let chemistry and pheromones get involved this early. End the date with a really tender handshake. Hold on to each other's hands for a long moment and look each other in the eye. This may sound corny, but if done with honesty it can convey real emotion.

After your pre-date, do not fall into the trap of second-guessing and doubting what every communication (or lack of communication) you receive from the other person means. Trust in God's plan for you. If this person is the one for you and you show up authentically, you will end up together. It really is as simple as that! Move forward with the confidence that things will work out exactly the way they should.

First "Official" Date

This official first date should be a bit more intimate than the pre-date. Dinner at a nice restaurant would be the ideal activity for this date. This will help you get to know this person more and begin to understand what he or she likes and dislikes. You can introduce alcohol at this point, but no more than one cocktail or a glass of wine each. When you have this fresh, excited energy coursing through your body and you add a bottle of wine to the mix, you may feel too uninhibited and act in a way that you wouldn't otherwise. The person you become after consuming a large amount of alcohol is not the authentic you who should be present throughout this date.

You can start to ask more serious questions and discuss slightly heavier topics. Many people say not to discuss religion or politics on a date, but I disagree with this. You want to learn everything about this person, especially their values. This will give you real insight into who they are. The last thing you want is to be blindsided by information after you're already in a relationship. You don't necessarily need to share the same opinions about these subjects to fall in love—perhaps you'll get into a heated, stimulating debate that you'll both really enjoy—but you do need to be respectful and nonjudgmental about your differences. If you can't even be real enough to share who you really are in the beginning without scaring one of you off, then there is your answer about moving to the next date. Be true to who you are and let the other person see the wonderful, authentic you!

Second Date

If you still feel connected to this person after the first date, go on another date that is somewhere a little bit off the beaten path. It's a really good idea to do something different on this date that will show you a completely different side of the other person's personality. Remember, you are both checking each other out to see if you can possibly be "the one." Some good ideas are a book reading, a church service, or a volunteer event. It's important that you each have your own interests, but you want to find commonalities and areas of mutual interest. Doing something together that you both enjoy will bond you more closely, and the experience will give you insight into how this person responds to different situations and people. You may gain a new appreciation for him or her, or you might realize that this isn't the person for you. Don't be too disappointed—that is completely okay, too! You are on the right path and have surely learned something from this dating experience.

If it goes well, this date should end with a warm hug. This may sound contrived, but there is a reason I am telling you to do this. I am giving you the best chance at beautiful, real love and trying to keep you away from the behaviors that have led to high divorce rates and unhappy marriages.

Third Date Onward

Continue to go on unique dates that will reveal different sides of your personalities. At this point, you should not be focused on the future or where this relationship is going. Simply enjoy each other's company and continue to get to know each other on a deeper and deeper level. You should go on at least eight to ten great dates before committing to each other, so don't worry about that right now. Go on dates that will really teach you something about the other person, not just to dinner and the movies. Your entire goal is to be your true self and get to know the other person's true self so that you can make a wise and informed decision about whether or not you were meant to be together.

By the fourth or fifth date, if you feel like it, you can kiss each other and begin to express your feelings this way. You may be tempted to get more intimate at this point, but I strongly encourage you to wait. A kiss can tell you so much about a person. If you are really feeling tempted, I want to paint a picture of the goal you are holding out for. My husband and I recently went to dinner and saw a very elderly couple sitting on the same side of a booth, holding tightly on to each other's hands over the table. Each of their other hands shook as they held their menus. Their age and ill health were obvious, but they were huddled close together, looking at each other with pure adoration in their eyes. They clearly shared a bond that was built on the true building blocks of love—a bond that could withstand time and the travesties of old age. This is what I want for you and it is so worth waiting for!

HOMEWORK ASSIGNMENT

Check In with Your Partner/Spouse

This homework assignment is for those of you who are married or in a relationship but may be struggling to experience the fullness of love that you are looking for. If you are not in a relationship now, read through the assignment and keep the advice fresh in your mind as you move on and begin to experience love in a relationship.

Otherwise, call your partner or spouse and ask for a mutually beneficial time within the next twenty-four hours to get together and relax, perhaps with a glass of wine. Sit down to discuss how life is going. This conversation doesn't need to be deep or heavy, unless it naturally goes there on its own! Take this time together to share what is happening in each of your worlds, as well as to discuss some fun ideas for your next date. Perhaps you can plan a weekend away, either far from home or nearby but at a great hotel!

Do not forget why you two fell in love in the first place! Keep it real, keep it fresh, and keep it sincere, sexy, and alive! You should be going out on dates together at least once a week. Lance and I have two date nights a week. It is a big part of what keeps our marriage alive, close, and fun. In fact, after fifteen years, I still get butterflies and excited when our next date is approaching!

CHAPTER TWELVE
Love Assessment

WHEN YOU BEGIN dating and looking for love, you must be ready to genuinely assess each person and potential relationship based on what you've learned throughout this process so that you will know when you have truly met the right one. This will also help you avoid making the same mistakes that you made in the past by settling or choosing to commit to someone who wasn't right for you. The first step toward committing to a partner is to stop dating other people. It may sound obvious, but many people continue dating multiple people for far too long, which only complicates and confuses the entire process. Remember, your goal is not to act like the next reality-show bachelor or bachelorette. You want to start experiencing real love, right now, and the best way to do that is to remain clear and confident on every step of your journey.

When you are first dating, especially online, you can set up a first date for every night of the week if that feels natural to you, but don't force it by doing this if it begins to feel like a job, because in time, it will. And please don't hesitate to let the person go after the first date if you don't feel something unique or special between you. Too many people will go on a second or even third date with someone they're not interested in just because they don't want to hurt the other person's feelings or are afraid there's no one better out there. If you're genuinely unsure, good for you for being open-minded. Go on a second date, but if you don't feel a real tug in your soul about this person after the second date, let him or her go! Simply say something like, "I know we're both looking for the right one and I think you're an incredible person, but I don't believe that we are right for each other." If they respond with any anger or resentment, this only supports the fact that you made the right decision. Thank them for their time and move on.

If you have been dating several people and become confused about who you really feel connected to, take a week off from dating any of them. During this time, make a checklist of what you like and don't like about each person. There are good and bad things about everyone. No one is perfect, but look at your lists and see if anything written there is a deal-breaker. A deal-breaker is something that goes against your value system, and if there are deal-breakers on any of your lists, those people are not right for you. As you narrow down your lists, ask God to guide you to the right person, and then ask yourself if you feel a pull toward one person more than another. Over the course of the week, weed out the people who you are ready to let go of and then move forward with complete confidence that you are making the right decision. Trust in yourself and trust in God, and there is no question that you will be led to the right person.

It is important not to get caught up in dating multiple people, because it can be very addictive, not to mention confusing, to have several people courting you at once. Never forget that your goal is to find your soul mate, not to feel the excitement or ego boost that may come with serial dating. It is important that you let someone go as soon as you realize that he or she is not meant for you—whether or not you are dating anyone else! This should certainly be by the second or third date, at the latest. Don't ever be afraid of having no one to date. This will keep you free and clear to meet the *right* one at the right time. When you decide to stop seeing someone, do not simply avoid or ignore them until they get the hint or let them know via e-mail or text that you won't be seeing them anymore. Make a plan to see them during the day and tell them responsibly and honestly that you don't think your time together is now. If they admit to feeling the same way, don't be offended! Remember, God is protecting you. It only makes sense that the other person would also feel that you two truly are not right for each other.

Should You Commit?

This may sound contradictory, but it is equally important not to commit to someone too soon. You should go on at least ten or twelve unique dates with someone before deciding to officially stop dating other people. After the fifth date but before you decide to commit to someone is the perfect time to get to know this person on many deeper levels. This is when you should begin to experience the world that surrounds the other person and start determining if this is a world that you could comfortably live in. Where does he spend most of his time? Who are her friends? What is his family like? Of course, you don't have to fit into his life seamlessly—perhaps you bring something unique to the mix that will improve his entire world or vice versa—but you do have to be genuinely comfortable with his lifestyle. Here are some of the best ways to find out whether or not this relationship is worth committing to.

Go to the Grocery Store

One easy way to find out a lot about this person is to go grocery shopping together. What does he or she eat? What do they put into their bodies? Do you both get excited about baking cookies together or experimenting with new spices that you've never heard of before? You don't have to like all of the same foods, but you should share an appreciation and respect for the other person's choices.

In one of my past relationships, we had a lot of fun together and focused on our similarities, but our first grocery store trip together presented a huge red flag that I unfortunately ignored. As we went up and down the aisles, I kept throwing little treats into the basket for us to enjoy together later, but he kept taking them out. When I finally asked him why, he said, "I'm not into sweets. They make you fat and your body is supposed to be a temple of God." This was too rigid for me, and I should have responded, "I agree with you, but I still like baking chocolate chip cookies from time to time," but instead I abandoned my true self and just went along with it. This may seem like a minor sticking point, but his rigidity in the grocery store translated into his being judgmental about everything that I put into my body throughout our relationship. He critiqued me all the time. When I finally gained the strength to say, "You can't tell me what to eat," it was too late. This was a thorn in our relationship that never would have existed if I had listened to my inner voice right away.

Never forget to love yourself first and be true to yourself during these dates. Again, if this person isn't the right one for you, that's okay. You must have faith that the right one will come along. If you are desperate to make things work and ignore warning signs, you will never be able to experience true love. At the same time, don't become overly critical of the other person's choices. You have to let them be him- or herself and love each other for who you are. If you do this, your differences won't matter so much and you will be able to come together over time to find things that you both enjoy.

Learn About His or Her Love Role Models

This is time to find out what this person learned about marriage and relationships when they were growing up. Don't make a big issue out of it, but bring it up naturally, as if you were asking any other question about their childhood. You can simply say, "Tell me about your parents. Would you want a marriage like theirs?" If they say yes, ask them why. What they say will tell you exactly what kind of marriage they want to have and in many ways how they will treat their spouse. There are specific things that you should be listening for, such as, "They respected each other," "They are great friends," "They always put each other first," "They had conflict but they always worked it out," or "Family was really important to them." These are clear signs that this person had good love role models and knows how to act in a healthy relationship.

If they say no, you should also ask why. Like it or not, this is what you're going to get with this person, too. As much as they may have healed or tried to overcome what they witnessed as a child, it is still a part of who they are. Trust me. Listen for things like, "My dad was kind of a jerk to my mom," "They fought like crazy," "They probably never should have been married," or "There wasn't any physical affection between them." In this case, have empathy. You are not there to judge. Say something like "That must have been really hard." If they respond to this by saying, "No, it wasn't hard at all. I just don't want the same thing in my own marriage," this is a clear sign that they are emotionally disconnected from their truth. If, however, they say, "Yes, it was hard. It was painful," take this opportunity to learn more. Ask, "What was painful about it?"

You want someone who is going to be real with you and willing to open up to you. Is this person safe to talk to? Can you communicate with them? We all naturally go into the same dynamics that we saw growing up. I am not saying that you should hold someone's parents' marriage against them. This person isn't their parents, but they took in a lot during their formative years. If they are connected enough to speak openly about it, that is a good sign. Later on, when you start to get more serious and begin taking each other for granted a little bit, the dynamic that they said they didn't like growing up will naturally start to come out. When this happens, it will help you to know that they will probably be willing to talk to you about it since they were open about it once before.

When this situation eventually occurs, ask them to sit down and talk, and start by saying something positive. One huge mistake that many women make is going right into their gripes and what their partner isn't doing correctly. Instead, start by thanking them for taking the time to talk to you, and come up with at least two or three things that they are doing really well. Do this from your heart, not just to sugarcoat the bad stuff. Then say something like, "Do you remember when we first met and we talked about our parents' marriages?" Keep it light, and tell him or her, "Honey, I'm kind of scared that we're going there. What do you think?"

You need this person to care about your concerns no matter how valid or invalid they are, and not get defensive and turn it on you. Those are major red flags. Maybe they will say something neutral like, "Really? I didn't notice. What are you noticing?" As long as you can continue talking it out, you are in a healthy place. Of course, you'll continue to have disagreements, but as long as you can talk through it and stay "comrades," you'll be fine. However, if they put up a wall and turn on you, then you need to think about packing up your emotions and taking a break. This doesn't mean that you have to break up, but you should definitely take a break and reassess.

Remember, when you get married, anything that's not working in your relationship will be amplified. If this person is coming from a place of healthy self-esteem, you can say just about anything and they won't get defensive or turn it on you. One of my clients recently called me and was really upset about a situation with one of her family members. She was yelling, "I can't believe that she said this to me!" I asked her, "Is what she said true?" She said, "Of course not." I told her that if it wasn't true, there was no reason to be so angry. If I told you that your skin was purple, you would know for certain that it wasn't true, but how would you respond? Would you become angry and hostile or just laugh it off and say, "It's kind of funny that you think I'm purple, but it's not true." The same principle applies to any type of confrontation. If your partner is healthy and open, anything that you say to him or her and vice versa will naturally be responded to with a desire to understand, along with love.

Is This the One?

If you have been dating someone exclusively for a while and feel like you've fallen in love, you may be wondering whether or not it's time to take the relationship to the next level. Here are some of my best tips for finding out if this person is really the one for you.

Hit the Road

This may sound strange, but before getting serious with a partner, I highly recommend going on a road trip together. You will learn so much about this person by seeing how they handle everything from road snacks to road rage, and this is all information that you need to have before getting seriously involved. The trip itself doesn't have to be across the country. Start out on a fun note by giving each other the assignment to come up with a few places that are about four hours away by car. Get together and present your ideas to each other, and then pick one together and plan your trip.

Don't discuss ahead of time what you're going to pack for the trip. You'll learn much more by seeing what he or she chooses to bring when left to his or her own devices. At the same time, you should show up with whatever you would normally pack for a road trip. You want to present nothing but your true, authentic self on every part of this trip. If you would normally bring a bag of chips to munch on in the car, bring that. If you would prefer to spend hours cutting up fresh veggies to bring, do that. Also bring your favorite music and some fun road games that you remember playing with your family as a kid. It's healthy and fun to bring child's play into your relationship at this point.

On the trip, your job (in addition to being your true self the whole time) is to pay attention. What is your reaction to this person's music choices? How does he or she handle traffic or the stress of getting lost? How hard or easy is it to agree on where to stop and eat? Are you having fun? Can you see yourself doing this for another forty years? Don't attach too much to any outcome. If you go on the trip feeling like it really, really needs to work, you won't be able to see things as they truly are. If the other person ends up driving you crazy or offending you in some way, be grateful for having this information now rather than feeling disappointed. This is God's way of protecting you from getting further involved with someone who is not right for you. At the same time, don't worry about impressing the other person or convincing him or her that you are the right one for them. Don't try to be anything other than what you really are. If your true self does manage to impress them, that is wonderful, but you can't force it.

After Lance and I met, we went on a road trip together. We were listening to "Staying Alive" by the Bee Gees and when the chorus came on, we both started singing along at the exact same time in a high-pitch falsetto. It was kind of dorky, but we really connected in that moment. What resonated with both of us wasn't just the fact that we did the same thing at the same time but that we were being ourselves and willing to risk humiliation by singing really goofily, really poorly, and really loudly!

Since I believe that you should wait until marriage to be intimate, I recommend that you each pay for your own hotel room. If everything is going well and you are really feeling connected and attracted to this person, you might be very tempted, but I strongly encourage you to keep sex off the table for now. The two of you can kiss and hug and snuggle, but maintain some boundaries. Think about the pain and expense of divorce and remember that I am trying to keep you from that. Trust me and my thousands of clients who have taught me that this is truly the right way to do it. Get a good meal in before you jump into dessert!

Think about Your Best Friend

Marriage should be the best experience you ever have when it comes to love or friendship. If you are thinking about marrying someone, hold an image in your mind of the best friend you've ever had in your life. It can be a childhood friend or someone who is in your life now, but it should be the person whom you feel completely connected to and safe with, someone you can be playful with and serious with, whom you can tell anything at all without any fear or hesitation. Think about that friendship and then ask yourself if you have that same thing with the person you are considering marrying. You can continue to have other dear and very close friends after you get married, but you must also have a strong friendship with your partner. This is what will sustain you.

Also look at your parents' marriage. Did they have a friendship like the one you were picturing? Remember that whatever they had, you will end up having in full, or at least to some degree, too. My clients fight me on that all the time—right up until they end up experiencing it themselves. Even if you come from a great background, you are going to experience brokenness on some level. It's not all going to be perfect. Challenges will come up, both internally and externally, but if you have a strong foundation of friendship, it will see you through the hard times and help you use them to make your relationship even stronger.

Look for Deal-Breakers

As I already mentioned, a deal-breaker is something that goes against your personal value system. Before getting serious with a partner, you need to ask yourself if he or she exhibits any behaviors that you consider to be deal-breakers. Be true to yourself and your beliefs when looking for deal-breakers; don't shift your values in order to make things work. You can challenge yourself to open your mind and think differently, but don't lose the presence of who you really are. If you notice any deal-breakers in your relationship or even any red flags that concern you, they must be confronted right away. The other person's reaction to what you say will tell you whether or not to move forward with them. Even if you are in love with someone, you can't ignore warning signs out of fear of losing them. This is not the way to honor and be true to yourself. You might feel that you are in love and have a good relationship, but if you are secretly hoping and praying that some really important things will change, this may not be the person for you.

Talk about Marriage

Too many people (especially women) say that they have found the person they want to marry, but are afraid to bring it up and risk being seen as desperate or needy. This is a huge mistake. If you feel like you want to be with this person for the rest of your life, you should be able to go to them without fear of rejection and talk about it. He or she should be your best friend and you should already know how he or she feels about marriage. If you are afraid of how they'll respond if you bring it up, that is a huge warning sign. Why are you afraid to talk about something as important as marriage with the person you love and believe you are ready to spend your life with?

If you are in this situation, you must go to the person and speak to them from the heart. Say, "I am totally in love with you." Tell them that you can see yourself spending your life with them and then ask, "What about you?" If they feel the same way, that's great, but you have to accept it if they aren't quite in the same place as you. Don't try to figure out how to make them love you more. You can't have desperation wrapped around love. If, however, you feel that you can't wait for the other person to feel ready for marriage, you can tell them honestly that you will have to move on if they are not ready. I do not believe in giving ultimatums in any sort of manipulative way, but you can give this person a chance to come back and say yes or no after you explain how you feel. Perhaps he will realize that he really is ready and can't picture his life without you, or maybe she will say that the time is not right and will let you go. Either way, trust that it is okay. By letting you go, he or she has given you a chance to go find the person who is truly right for you. This is a gift. Remember, you cannot force love, and if you do force something that doesn't fit, it breaks.

Marriage's Best Chance

If you decide to marry this person, you will need to move forward with joy, trust, and love in your heart and with the determination and presence of mind to protect your marriage from becoming vulnerable throughout the years. Here are some of the most important ways to give your marriage the best chance at success once you have truly found the right person for you.

Have Faith

Throughout your marriage, challenges will come up, and the bond of your faith is a crucial part of your foundation. You need to have something bigger than the two of you that you can turn to when things get tough. Right now, you don't know what your story will be. In your marriage, you might go through cancer together. You might lose a child together. Maybe you'll have each other for only a year. Or perhaps you'll have ten healthy, wonderful children and a long, fruitful life together. As your story unfolds, you must ask God to guide you together. If you trust and have faith, his plan for you is far greater than anything you can stir up for yourself. When you don't trust and veer off your path, He will let you stumble and get hurt, but He will always be waiting for you to come back. This is something Lance and I have experienced many times and couldn't be more grateful for, regarding God's love and his lessons. The bottom line is that if you lose your way in your marriage, reconnect to God and He will help you get back on the right path.

Avoid Temptation

Temptation is a real and natural thing, and something that you most likely will face at some point in your marriage, no matter how much in love or truly committed you may be. I have very strict rules about avoiding temptation, and they are based on hundreds of stories I have heard over the years from both men and women about affairs starting innocently, even when everything in their marriage was going well. My first rule to avoid temptation is that you and your partner should not maintain any friendships with exes, unless you share a child and have to be healthy co-parents. Otherwise, you can stay friends in your heart and wish them all the love in the world, but there is no reason to spend time with them, have them in your lives, meet them for lunch, or even be friends with them on Facebook.

This may sound harsh or ridiculously rigid, but if the idea

makes you feel uncomfortable, you must ask yourself why. The people who fight me on this point the most are almost always the ones who end up admitting that their ex is there as a saving grace or that their friends of the opposite sex are a good escape just in case the marriage doesn't work out. If your partner refuses to cut off an ex-girlfriend or -boyfriend, this is a deal-breaker not only because of what that friendship might turn into but because it means that he or she is not putting you, the sanctity of your relationship, and your feelings first. For the same reasons, I believe that you should not have any *friends* of the opposite sex at all—that is, ones that you "hang out" with. Even the most innocent friendship can turn into something more under the right circumstances, and the truth is that every male client I've spoken to has told me that he would sleep with his female friends under the "right" circumstances, such as too much alcohol, emotional confusion, and so on. Many of them already have. We humans are sexual beings. There is no reason to tempt ourselves any more than we already are biochemically.

Another way to avoid temptation is to stop going out to bars with your friends. I have a lot of girlfriends who get all dressed up for girls' night and go out to the bars, but this can become too tempting a situation. You can enjoy a cocktail at a restaurant, but people in bars are typically either looking for love or looking to get drunk. If you are married, you shouldn't be looking for either one! I so often hear about affairs that started this way. A woman is in a wonderful marriage and goes out to a bar with a friend. A man approaches her with a notably flirtatious style and they strike up a conversation. They exchange cards, using the excuse of networking, and he e-mails her later. A friendship develops, and then one day, after fighting with her husband, she reaches out to him. The next thing she knows, she's having an emotional and then physical affair and doesn't understand what happened. The truth is that she shouldn't have been in that bar to begin with nor accepted a card from a gentleman who was clearly flirting with her. You have to protect what you have and take responsibility.

If you are married and find yourself becoming tempted by someone else, it means that there are things you either aren't getting from your partner, or, to be honest, that you haven't healed within yourself. How can you tell the difference between a natural attraction to someone and a true temptation? It is normal to notice people and even find them attractive, but if your marriage is healthy, your mind effortlessly moves on to the next thought after noticing them. If you can't stop staring or start to feel lonely and find yourself seeking attention from the other person, that is a sign that something is wrong within your marriage. Pay attention and check in with yourself to find out what is going on. Sit in a quiet spot and ask yourself, "Why am I feeling this? Is there something that I'm avoiding that doesn't feel good in my marriage? Am I afraid to be honest with myself about a disconnect? What am I afraid of?" Don't shame yourself for feeling this way. It is your connection to God warning you to be careful and telling you that you need to get in touch with something, that there's more room for healing. We have all of the answers within us, so don't stop seeking until you have uncovered the truth.

Cleave to Your Spouse

I do believe that, as the Bible says, when a man marries he leaves his mother and father and cleaves to his wife. Once you are married, what you have known as your family becomes secondary, and your family is now what you create in your marriage. Your marriage must be honored that way, and your partner's needs must come before your parents' or siblings'. It is too easy for other family members to come in and penetrate your relationship unless these boundaries are firmly established from the beginning.

Have Fun

Your marriage should inspire you to be a better person and to see more of the world. It should bring you true joy. Mine does! You should look at life together as an adventure that you are facing as a team. That is what love is supposed to be and feel like. However, that doesn't mean that it always comes easily. You must each be aware and a bit methodical about staying strong and true to yourselves and your marriage so that you can each be there for each other. You can't afford to have a marriage that just exists. It's so easy to buy into a rut and think that your marriage is doomed. It takes work to combat that.

Share new experiences, and don't let yourselves begin to take each other for granted. The minute you do, disconnect will set in for each of you. Check in with yourself regularly and ask yourself if you've been taking your partner for granted. When was the last time you left a love note on the mirror for him to see in the morning? Have you flirted with him lately? What could you do to surprise him or make his day a little bit brighter? When was the last time you told him that you appreciate him? A marriage that is joyful, loving, fresh, and alive will be your reward for the work you put in!

HW

HOMEWORK ASSIGNMENT
Imagine Your Marriage

Once you have had a chance to absorb the lessons in this chapter, grab your journal and write down as specifically as possible what you see for yourself and desire when it comes to your experience with your spouse. How will you spend your time together as well as apart in the early days of your relationship? What about when children or grandchildren come around? Will you travel? Where and how? How do you want life to be when you are in your later years? Will you be holding hands and walking together side by side? Take the time to envision it—all of it. Write it down, pray for it, and call it to you.

FIVE-DAY LOVE REALITY CHECK

You now know how to approach dating for the absolute best chance of success and assess potential romantic partners along the way. Take a moment to just think of how far you've come since picking up this book! Doesn't it feel great to know that love surrounds you at every moment? You are only five days away from fully becoming the new, loving, authentic version of you—the person you were always meant to be. If you haven't yet met the person you've been waiting for, trust that he or she *is* coming and that the two of you are already connected. He or she is likely thinking of you at the same moment that you are thinking of him or her, and is just as eager and excited to meet you! Enjoy each day of your transformation as you look forward to experiencing real love together.

DAYS 26–30

CHAPTER THIRTEEN

Be the Loving Kind

NO MATTER HOW much you may have healed or how love-ready you may be, you will not be able to experience the wholeness of love until you begin to live a loving life in every way. Love is found not only between a man and a woman or in romance. As you know, I believe that love is the most pure, healing energy in the world, and we can call love to us by acting with love in every part of our lives. The energy that we put out not only has an impact on ourselves and those around us. It can change the world around us. If we allow our broken egos to send out hateful, negative energy, we become disconnected from one another and our entire society suffers. But when we are full of God's love and share it with the world, beauty and healing can be found.

The show *Lovetown, USA* was an experiment on the energy and power of love. It began with one simple question—what would happen if an entire town focused on nothing but love for thirty days? What would change? What would remain the same? If change did occur, how drastic would it be and far would it reach? I had the opportunity to be a part of this experiment, and it taught me that love's true power is even stronger than I had thought. All the experts on the show came on board with open hearts and minds but also with some skepticism about whether or not it would even work. The truth is that we had no idea what would happen. Maybe nothing would change or the changes would only be temporary, until the cameras stopped rolling and production on the show shut down.

Before we arrived, the town of Kingsland, Georgia, was fraught with tensions and negativity. Feuds had been going on for generations between families and even between congregations. The single people in the town felt lonely and hopeless. Marriages were suffering and children were being bullied in school. Unfortunately, none of this is exceptional. All of it is far too common in every town across the country. What was exceptional, however, is what happened after the experiment started. The show challenged the town to focus on nothing but love for thirty days. That included helping the singles to become love-ready and also involved community members supporting one another, families reconciling, town leaders setting aside grudges, and the community chipping in to help those in need.

From the first town meeting, in which we asked community

members to make suggestions about how the town could act more loving, I could feel a major shift taking place. Just thinking about the possibilities brought peace and joy to these people. It takes only one conscious act of love to get healing started! We encouraged them to focus on what they could do in their own lives to spread love, and it caught on like wildfire. Before long, the town bullies were showing up asking how they could get involved. Their pain was coming to the surface and they were starting to want something better for themselves. Families who hadn't spoken in years put aside their differences and reconnected. The churches that had been feuding came together for the good of the community. None of this was fabricated for the sake of the show. In fact, the town has kept it going on its own long after the cameras stopped rolling.

During filming one day, I noticed that one of the crew members was getting choked up. I asked him what he was feeling and he said to me, "I feel like this is changing my life just from filming it." He went on to tell me about his ex-wife, who had cheated on him and ended their marriage. While he had been holding on to resentment and anger toward her for all these years, observing the changes that were taking place in Kingsland helped him realize his own part in the destruction of his marriage. He said, "I'm beginning to understand why she did it and there's a part of me that now wants to forgive her." The loving energy in the town was so powerful that it was helping him to heal from his divorce. By forgiving his ex-wife, he was finally able to move on and live a happy, loving life.

Never forget that we are what we attract and we attract what we are. If we are the loving kind, we attract love, but if we are not loving, we repel love from our lives. Whether you are single or married, making love your focus will help you experience love of the highest level. This may sound surreal, but the show's experiment proves that it is true. We can all create our own Lovetown by focusing on love in our own lives and in our own towns. I have pulled out some of the lessons that we learned while filming *Lovetown, USA* so that you can take the "loving kind" challenge and transform your own life by focusing on love.

Hold a "Town Hall" Meeting

In Kingsland, we held a literal town hall meeting, but you can do this yourself by deciding exactly what the "town hall" is in your life. Gather your family or closest friends together and talk about what is *really* going on. What is feeling broken? How can you all act more loving toward one another? Keep the focus on healing and get organized by delegating specific tasks to each person. You will be amazed by the level of change that you can accomplish just by starting with the truth and putting out a different energy. Begin with yourself and your family and then branch out to your town or city and move on to a literal town hall. Our entire world is in desperate need of more of this healing energy and you can truly make a difference by spreading your own loving ways.

Pay Attention

You can start to be the loving kind by giving of yourself to others in the form of your focus and attention. We all get so caught up in our own lives that we often ask each other, "How are you?" without even noticing what response we get from the other person. The next time you ask someone how they are, ask it with sincerity and pay attention to their answer. Perhaps they will say that they are fine but their face won't match their words. People are suffering in silence all around us, and if they feel the sincerity of your inquiry, they might be inspired to open up to you. Take the extra step of checking in with the reality of the people around you. Showing that you care and that people matter is incredibly powerful and healing. Learn how to slow down and really listen to people. Are you really listening to your children and what they are trying to say to you? Many of us are so caught up in our own lives that we appease one another with pat words instead of really connecting, but our spouses, friends, and especially children pick up on that dismissive energy. Stop hurrying people throughout the day and start taking the time to listen and fully respond to them.

One thing that I am personally trying to do more is to ask people in service positions how *they* are when they rattle off their rehearsed, "How are you?" I have found that when I ask this with sincerity, their entire energy shifts and becomes more positive. This is such a simple thing that you can do to brighten someone's day.

Pay It Forward

Paying it forward simply means going out of your way to improve someone's day. This can be on a small or large scale. If you are at a drive-through Starbucks, why not give the attendant a few extra dollars to pay for coffee for the person in the car behind you? You have no idea what that person is going through. Maybe he is battling depression or feeling lonely. Even if she's having a great day, this gesture will make it even better. It can change someone's entire mood and energy if they feel like someone else cares enough to make a difference in their day. Never forget that you have the power to do this.

Start to look for opportunities every day to help others. The next time you're in line at the grocery store and notice that someone forgot their credit card, offer to pay for their groceries (if you're in a financial position to do so). Gather up the extra jars and cans of food in your house and bring them to a local food bank. Chances are that you won't miss these items, but they will make a big difference to someone else. Find other, nonmonetary, ways of giving back by showing up to volunteer and connect with people who are suffering nearby.

Conquer Drama Addictions

I believe that drama is an addiction that adds so much negativity to our lives. This may sound strange, but drama can have a similar effect on the brain as drugs or alcohol. With a drama addiction, the brain's chemistry becomes dependent on the chemicals that are released when they indulge in gossip, anger, or other dramatic behaviors. This is just like a drug addict who becomes dependent on a substance's effect on the brain. Our brains can trick us into believing that we need certain things in order to feel "normal," but this is actually a heightened, unhealthy version of normal. When people become addicted to drama, they are either dependent on other people's reaction to them or on their own reactions to others. When they get or create the desired reaction, "fight or flight" hormones are released, creating a high. The person suddenly feels better without even realizing what is happening. Then when they feel lonely or bored, they will drum up fights or gossip in order to feel those "normalizing" chemicals.

You cannot live a truly loving life if you are addicted to drama, because drama is inherently negative. If you feel that you may be suffering from a drama addiction, know that you can create the same sense of calm, and in a healthier way than the drama now gives you. This is when real healing and transformation can take place. The next time you feel yourself getting caught up in a cycle of drama, take a breath and just stop. Don't do anything to perpetuate the drama. Stop yourself from reacting to someone else's drama and go do something nice for yourself. Take a bubble bath, meditate, or pray.

We have so much more control over ourselves and our lives than we even realize. Every day, we can choose how we react to others and the energy that we send out into the universe. Instead of rushing to judgment or anger, we can choose to be the loving kind by taking a moment to question and process what is being said and why. Just recently, Lance and I were on the verge of a major fight when he was acting a bit brusque with me. I was tempted to snap back and say, "how dare you speak to me that way," but instead of being so quick to react, I held back and asked him, "What's wrong? Are you feeling okay?" He responded by opening up to me about some things that he was feeling insecure about, and it helped us connect and feel closer than ever. You may think that you are exerting power by standing up to someone, but the real power comes from acting with love instead of reacting with anger.

Practice Compassion

We can make the biggest shift in our lives by seeking to understand why pain is occurring and move forward with peace and understanding rather than blame or shame. The healing power of love can be extended to others in countless ways if you treat them with compassion at every opportunity. When dealing with someone who is rude, it's so easy to think, "How dare he?" It is human nature for our minds to go there, but we can't stay in that place of blame and negativity. We must slow down and find compassion. In these situations, take a moment to back up and wonder where the rude behavior is coming from. You don't know what someone is dealing with at home or in their lives. Our instincts are often to protect ourselves, but it is more important to focus on understanding where the other person is coming from.

This can be a difficult thing to master, and it is something that many of us struggle with. My client Alicia recently told me about an experience she had at the emergency room with her daughter. The woman who was filling out the intake forms was incredibly rude to her, acting as if her daughter was an enormous nuisance rather than a patient in need. Alicia's initial instinct was to protect her daughter, and it was a struggle for her to hold herself back from anger. She took a breath and reminded herself that she had no idea what kind of day this woman was having. Maybe she had an abusive spouse or a parent with a life-threatening illness. Alicia looked for something to genuinely compliment her on and settled for saying, in a very kind voice, "Wow, you are so thorough. Everyone should be as dedicated to their jobs as you." Before Alicia knew it, the woman's entire demeanor had changed. Suddenly she was smiling and finding ways to help Alicia's daughter avoid a long wait. This is a real testament to the power of love and shows that Alicia has become successful at leading a truly loving life.

Never Lose Hope

It is essential to never forget that love and marriage can be amazing, and that life can be happy and joyful no matter what you've been through. Look at what I've come from and the experiences I've walked through in my life. I am a true, living, breathing example of being able to achieve whatever you believe in your heart, despite the obstacles. If you fill your heart with loving energy, you can heal from anything. Every bit of brokenness in this world is based on a pain that hasn't been healed. This may sound negative, but it is actually quite positive because it means that every bit of pain that is out there represents an opportunity for healing. All it takes is attention and effort.

I had the honor and pleasure of being able to work with Oprah, and I am always inspired by how far she's come since childhood in her own journey of healing. People sometimes see Oprah as a successful tycoon and forget where she came from, but as she has shared with the public, she came, at times, from a very deep level of brokenness. Despite her childhood, as she has shared, she always followed something inside her that was guiding her, and she clearly still has a beautiful piece of humility inside of her that is pure and keeps her on her path to bring a higher level of hope to our society. Her story always reminds me of love's remarkable power.

I want to end this book by reminding you one last time that the energy of love has the power to heal. By acting from love, living a loving life, and holding love in our hearts, we can change the world, every last one of us. If each of us read from this book every day and then put it down and took a moment to send love out to the universe, together we would make an impact. Why not start now? After reading these last words, take a moment to thank God for His love and ask Him to help you send this loving energy out to those around you. Through this simple act, you will bring yourself and the whole world one step closer to the exquisite experience of love.

HOMEWORK ASSIGNMENT
Rewrite Your Story

At the beginning of the book, I asked you to write the story of your life thus far, and I want you to do the same thing now but with all of the additional knowledge, love, and wisdom that you've gained from this book. Without going back to read what you wrote the first time, write a new version of your life story. When you are done, go back and read both versions and notice the differences. What has been revealed about your childhood? What have you learned about your dysfunctions and where they came from? Most important, what have you discovered about your true self and what love means to you? What do you now see and accept for your future when it comes to experiencing love?

FIVE-DAY LOVE REALITY CHECK

I am so glad to have taken this journey of love with you! Thank you for trusting me with your heart, and I congratulate you on all that you have accomplished. By now you should be experiencing a feeling of peace, love, freedom, and a loving connection with yourself that you've never felt before. I hope you have learned that love does not elude you and never has. Hopefully you sense that love is all around you! As you move forward, continue to feel the amazing love that not only surrounds you, but that you actually are made of. This has been a journey, a field trip toward love, and there is still more to come—more learning, growing, healing, and transforming, all with great gifts waiting just for you. Gather all that you've learned, take it in with a deep, cleansing breath, and know that the experience of love you've always hoped for is waiting just outside your door. Believe in it and go get it! See you there!